OVERCOMING FEAR

50 Lessons on Being Bold and Living the Dream

Joe Serio, Ph.D.

Show fear who's boss!

Best wishes!

Joe

Project Manager: Jennifer Serio
Design Team: Harriet Brewster and Jena Rodriguez

Printed in the United States of America
ISBN 13: 978-0-9900216-1-2

www.LEDtraining.com

Contents

PART 2
ASSESSMENT MECHANISMS

PART 3
ACTION MECHANISMS

The long span of the bridge of your life is supported by countless cables called habits, attitudes, and desires. What you do in life depends upon what you are and what you want. What you get from life depends upon how much you want it, how much you are willing to work and plan and cooperate and use your resources. The long span of the bridge of your life is supported by countless cables that you are spinning now, and that is why today is such an important day. Make the cables strong!

~ L.G. Elliott

About the *Get the Nerve*™ *Series*

The idea for the *Get the Nerve*™ *Series* grew out of my personal transformation from being fearful of most things to facing that fear and achieving more than I thought possible.

My goal is to share what I have learned so that you, too, can see the possibility for your own life and make it a reality.

Each book in the series begins with reflections on fear. This builds the foundation for the following lessons, which are specific to the topic of each book. As L.G. Elliott says in the quotation on the facing page, "Your life is supported by countless cables called habits, attitudes, and desires." This series is a blueprint for helping you create and strengthen the cables of your bridge, so you can live the most inspired life you can imagine.

I would love to hear about changes you make in your life as a result of the *Get the Nerve*™ *Series*. Please contact me with your stories of personal transformation at drjoe@joeserio.com.

Other Titles in
the *Get the Nerve*™ *Series*

Public Speaking: 50 Lessons on Presenting Without Losing Your Cool

Time Management: 50 Lessons on Finding Time for What's Important

For more information about these titles in this series, please visit us at www.LEDtraining.com

Introduction

For, usually and fitly, the presence of an introduction
is held to imply that there is something of
consequence and importance to be introduced.

~ Arthur Machen

What are we afraid of? What is keeping us from going after our goals, developing great relationships, and living our best life?

So often we psych ourselves out and give in to defeat even before we get started. The chatterbox voices in our heads give us plenty of justification not to be bold and live the dream: We're not good enough. We'll make a mistake. Others will make fun of us. And on and on.

I was paralyzed for a very long time by my internal, negative chatterbox. I suffered through school with anxiety. I had terrible relationships. I wasted countless hours in front of the television. I was fearful of making mistakes. I was fearful of not being enough. I was fearful of being left alone. I failed at being bold.

I spent so much time fearful of being rejected by others I didn't realize I was rejecting myself.

Over the years I figured out that, while it's important to have clear goals, it's absolutely critical to create an effective process to reach those goals. I created countless mechanisms within the process to change habits and work more efficiently.

But the process is not just a means to reach the specific goal you set for yourself. The process is the place magic happens.

The process is the place you allow yourself to imagine what's possible.

The process is the place that shows you how to take the first steps.

The process is the place you face yourself and realize, "Yes, I can!"

The process is the place you discover greater inner peace and become who you really are.

The mechanisms in this book are the means to get you into the process, to experience magic, and to begin to become your true self.

Remember, it's like Thomas Jefferson said, "If you want something you've never had, you must be willing to do something you've never done."

What is "living the dream"? It's more than just "living our dreams" in the sense of accomplishing things or getting everything we want.

The dream is getting off our own backs, creating a life of peace, and finding our own voice, the expression of what's truly in our heart.

Living the dream means enjoying a connection to yourself, those around you, and to your spiritual foundation that is honest, loving, meaningful, and, most of all, fear-less. To me, that is an ideal worth pursuing, and it makes all the difference.

How to Use This Book

Overcoming Fear: 50 Lessons on Being Bold and Living the Dream is a practical guide of mechanisms to help you develop your own system for overcoming fear. And it doesn't matter if your fears are centered on money, career, relationships, health, or anything else.

This book is arranged in five parts.

Part I, About Fear, provides context for the book and helps create a mindset you'll use to approach your fear. It is the foundation for the remainder of the book.

Part II, Assessment Mechanisms, is meant to help you establish a baseline. What is your starting point? What is the reality you find yourself in? What are the facts of your life as it now looks?

Part III, Action Mechanisms, outlines practical exercises you can use every day to deal with fear.

Part IV, A Seven-Step Success Plan for Overcoming Fear, gathers the earlier lessons into an effective and easy-to-follow plan.

Part V, Living the Dream, rounds out the book with a wonderful success story about what's possible when you break through the walls that keep you from getting beyond your comfort zone.

While you could read *Overcoming Fear* in any order, I recommend reading it from beginning to end. There is an arc, a logical progression, to the lessons.

The benefits you will get from reading – and applying – the lessons in this book cannot be fully described. You must experience it. You will see shifts you never thought possible. You will gain perspective you've never had. You will notice improvement in virtually every area of your life. But it's up to you. No one else can do it for you.

In a nutshell, this book is about you. Everything you need to overcome fear is inside you. The mechanisms I've laid out will help you bring those things out. If you find this process easy, you're probably not doing it right. You will have to ask some difficult questions of yourself and face some painful realities. That's ok. That's normal. But the work is doable, and it's worth it.

Master the lessons in this book, and you will change your life, learn to be bold, and live the dream.

Part 1

About Fear

Lesson 1

The Fear List

*The greatest mistake a man can make is to be afraid
of making one.*

~ Elbert Hubbard

*Failure is an inescapable part of life and a critically
important part of any successful life.*

~ Tal Ben-Shahar

Ask others what they are afraid of, and frequently the initial responses we receive include spiders, snakes, heights, and the dentist.

Probe a little deeper, and the list of fears becomes more delicate, more sensitive, and more profound. Facial expressions change to reveal more intimate secrets. People appear more childlike, as if they are being transported to an earlier moment in time when those fears were initially experienced. At the same time, they look weary from hanging on to those fears for a very long time.

As we ask more people, the list becomes predictable and very familiar.

- Fear of making mistakes
- Fear of rejection
- Fear of embarrassment
- Fear of criticism
- Fear of losing approval/love
- Fear of losing control

- Fear of failure
- Fear of success

The problem, of course, isn't the presence of fear. The problem is how we handle fear, what we do with it. There are plenty of successful men and women who feel fear but are not fearful. They are not paralyzed by fear.

In the list above, the focus of power and energy in most of those fears lies with someone else. We give away our power, worrying about what others will think of us, letting them judge us and determine our paths, instead of living life on our own terms.

For example, if I still let fear of criticism control me, I probably wouldn't have been able to risk writing this book.

Fortunately, I was able to move beyond the paralysis. It took a change of mind and heart and good, practical mechanisms (Lesson 22) to get the nerve to muster the courage. Now I can write what I know, in the hope it serves you in some small way. And the fact that not everyone will like the book or agree with it is OK with me.

It's natural to pay attention to what others think of us; we don't want to be kicked out of the tribe.

But when we start to obsess about it, and every decision we make is based on the fear of losing the approval of others, the process becomes problematic. Paralysis can result, depriving us of our ability to work effectively, play passionately, be bold, and live the dream.

TAKEAWAY: If you change your mind, you can change your life.

Handling Fear

We fear something before we hate it; a child who fears noises becomes a man who hates noises.

~ Cyril Connolly

How we relate to fear determines how we do in life, and maybe it is the essence of who we are.

~ Thom Rutledge

What is our fear saying to us? If we look at the list of fears in Lesson 1, we could summarize it as "I can't handle it."

- I can't handle the possibility of being embarrassed.
- I can't handle the possibility of being criticized.
- I can't handle the possibility of being rejected.
- I can't handle the possibility of failing.

Our response to this mantra of "I can't handle" frequently is to give mediocre performances instead of our best or simply not try at all. We're too busy protecting ourselves. We're so afraid of the possibility of pain that we treat it as though it's guaranteed.

I spent years "protecting myself" from the possibility of criticism and failure. I focused on my shortcomings, my imperfections, and the opinions of others. I convinced myself I couldn't handle most things. That which we focus on becomes reality.

The sad part is my imagination was full of wonderful things I wanted to do and be.

It doesn't require a sudden, dramatic event in our lives to make us believe we can't handle it. It's already happened, slowly, subtly. We created the responses a long time ago every time we thought we couldn't handle something, every time we thought we weren't good enough. Every time we thought we weren't worthy of love.

We play these responses over and over again in our heads.

The protective layers built up over the years have pushed in the walls of our comfort zone closer and closer to the point where we don't want to risk very much or take too many chances, if any. In many cases, those walls have also become so thick that breaking through them can be difficult.

Facing fear means starting to understand we can handle much more than we believe we can.

Facing fear means crafting for ourselves a new story about our past, one that changes our beliefs, our assumptions, our thoughts, and our responses.

Facing fear also means we need to create mechanisms to make it much easier for us to face our darker, less generous selves.

We deal with fear not by dancing around it or eliminating it, but by going through it – having courage to act not in the absence of fear but in spite of it. We won't do it unless we have a plan with the right tools to build effective mechanisms to live the dream.

Contrary to what we might be feeling, we don't have to go it alone, we don't have to reinvent the wheel, and we don't have to suffer in silence while we kill our own chances for happiness in life. We're almost never the very first person to walk our chosen path. We can handle it.

TAKEAWAY: It's time to change our perception of what we can handle.

Overcoming Fear

The only thing we have to fear is fear itself.

~ Franklin D. Roosevelt

The only thing we have to fear is the fear of fear itself.

~ Thom Rutledge

There are those who believe fear is a great motivator of others, that people will respond with their best only when threats are issued or punishment is implied. These threats frequently result in fear of harsh criticism and embarrassment.

That is, the potential for suffering is part of the "motivation."

The problem with this approach is that, while it may result in some short-term action, the use of fear in order to motivate very often intensifies the fear in the person receiving it. It doesn't help develop self-esteem, self-motivation, discipline, or peace in the receiving party.

Once a person becomes fearful – conditioned by the actions and attitudes of fear-inducing people – that person carries a disproportionate concern about acceptance from others. Will they approve of me? Will they yell at me? Will they punish me for stepping out of line? Will they give me a second chance?

The person on the receiving end will then not act from a place of giving or out of seeing potential possibility, but rather from a position of lack, weakness, and, of course, fear.

Think about your own life. Has a parent or manager led with an iron fist? Did that create a healthy environment?

This isn't to say that some acceptance by others isn't important, but if our concern about their opinion is so powerful that our fear prevents us from acting, then there's a problem.

At the other end of the spectrum, there are some who believe a complete absence of fear is possible and desirable. This is a wonderful perspective; perhaps it is possible to live a life totally absent of fear. In my opinion, few are able to attain that level of inner peace.

I'm not particularly interested in either end of the spectrum. I believe punishment or the constant threat of punishment serves to instill or deepen fear. By the same token, if we think the absence of fear is necessary before acting, we wouldn't get anything done.

In my life, the presence of my father was so strong that even years after he died, I was making decisions and judging my life according to whether I thought he would approve or not.

When I finally put into perspective my fear of punishment – by using the mechanisms in this book, I was able to change my life and go after what I wanted on my terms. "Overcoming" in this book does not mean we will never feel fear. It is closer to the classic definition of courage – the ability to act in spite of fear.

The goal is to get us moving in a way that we can advance our lives without being paralyzed by the opinions of others – past, present, or future. And we want to do so in a way in which we're not constantly looking over our shoulder for the hammer of punishment to come down upon us – whether from someone else or ourselves.

TAKEAWAY: Instilling fear in ourselves and others does not produce the best results.

Moving Forward

The best way out is always through.

~ Helen Keller

Love is what we were born with.
Fear is what we learned here.

~ Marianne Williamson

In our mind's eye, we can sometimes look at the big picture, the totality of what we're trying to accomplish, and bury ourselves in fear.

So often we find our initial responses to fear unwarranted. We allow the fear to dictate how we proceed. Before long, we get past the fear and address the task at hand. When we push fear to the side, we find the task being accomplished much quicker than anticipated.

As always, we have a choice. We can allow fear to prevent us from doing things we dream about, or we can find a way to manage our fear and move forward into things we never dreamed possible.

When we realize everyone – even the most successful among us – has fear, we'll find it easier to move forward.

When we realize perfectionism – not to be confused with excellence – has no role in the creative process, we'll find it easier to move forward.

When we realize the universe is rooting for our success, we'll find it easier to move forward.

When we realize all creativity – life itself – is about taking small steps on a daily basis, here and now, in this minute, we'll find it easier to move forward.

It is useful to reframe how we think about fear. It doesn't take advanced degrees or special talent. Awareness and effective mechanisms introduced into our daily lives will help dramatically reduce the impact of fear and increase our productivity, our confidence, and our satisfaction.

Here are useful ways to reframe our thoughts about fear:

- Understand the difference between healthy fear and paralyzing fear.
- Realize fear can be a result of interpretations of events from childhood, a time when we weren't qualified to accurately interpret what was actually happening around us.
- Resist the urge to compare how we feel on the inside to how others behave on the outside. It may appear others are fearless. They're not.
- Create mechanisms, games, and psychological tricks to counteract the fear that creeps up inside of us.
- Develop the habit of preparing well for whatever we set out to do. Proper preparation prevents poor performance – and goes a long way to reduce fear.
- Don't try to complicate or overthink our task. Just the opposite – KISS: Keep It Super Simple.
- Understand that perfectionism and procrastination are traps keeping us from living *our* lives.
- Do our best to serve others. When we serve, we can enhance our appreciation for what we have and our empathy for others. We put our fear in perspective when we get out of our own heads and engage with others.

TAKEAWAY: Overcoming fear and moving forward is the foundation for living the dream.

The Ally and the Bully

You are 100% responsible for your life.

~ Unknown

Be in charge of your life.
Forget about being in control.

~ Thom Rutledge

Are you an expert procrastinator? Are you easily embarrassed? Are you a perfectionist? Do you feel guilty about saying no? Do you worry about what others will say about you? Do you believe your worth as a person is tied to your performance?

Most of us can identify with at least one of these questions, and probably more. I know all of these things applied to me.

These feelings and beliefs rest on a foundation of fear. Our avoidance, judgment, prejudice, shame, guilt, control, agitation, perfectionism, anger, and countless other emotions, thoughts, and behaviors are hints we are profoundly afraid of something.

Let's distinguish from the outset that not all fear is bad.

Positive fear has been helping us survive for thousands of years.

This fear tells us to be careful, warns us about dangers in our environment, and cues us about a heightened sense of attention in certain situations. That has been referred to as natural fear, positive fear, or, as psychotherapist Thom Rutledge calls it, the "Ally."

The Ally is a voice we need to cultivate. There are some who may do us harm and situations that could lead to physical danger. As Gavin De Becker implores us in his classic book, *The Gift of Fear,* we must pay attention to the hairs on the back of our neck. We have wonderful systems for protecting ourselves when it's imperative.

The negative fear is referred to as neurotic fear, or the "Bully," as Rutledge calls it.

We create this fear ourselves, and it has little to do with physical survival. This is the fear generated by messages in our environment that we have been interpreting since birth. We have been watching, listening, and trying to make sense of the world around us and our place in it. This book is about that fear.

I spent the better part of my life misinterpreting my parents, siblings, teachers, peers, neighbors, the media, religious figures, and countless others. I took their opinions and perspectives to heart and used their words to draw conclusions about myself. I created the Bully voice in my chatterbox head, and negated much of what is splendid about myself.

The Bully keeps many of us focused on our faults. As the medieval Persia poet Sa'di said in his metaphor, "People are crying up the rich and variegated plumage of the peacock, and he is himself blushing at the sight of his ugly feet."

Like the Ally, the Bully also thinks it is protecting us. But, this protection – from embarrassment, from mistakes, from rejection, from failure – keeps us from living our true purpose to the fullest extent. It keeps us wrapped in the warm cocoon of our comfort zone and makes our lives smaller than they could be, robbing us of our happiness.

The temptation is great to try to impress people, be validated by them, or live our lives according to their beliefs. We're also tempted to blame them for the way our lives turn out. But, in the end, we're the only ones responsible for our lives.

TAKEAWAY: Build a strong Ally and put the Bully in perspective.

Fear is a Head Game

Avoidance is the disease. Non-avoidance is the cure.

~ Unknown

Fears are educated into us, and can, if we wish,
be educated out.

~ Karl Menninger

If we let go of an object, it will drop to the floor. If we drop the object ten times, it will drop to the floor each of those ten times.

Nothing in the way we drop the object, nothing in the way we think about the way it falls, will change the fact that it falls. It is a physical law. We can't change gravity.

But most issues pertaining to fear are not scientific in the same way gravity is. Here we're not interested in neurology or brain chemistry, although of course they play a role in fear. We're more interested in the stories we have told ourselves and the possibility of changing them.

More than that, we're interested in creating mechanisms necessary to move forward, in spite of existing fear, not necessarily in its absence.

In this lesson, we want simply to bring to the front of our minds the idea that, outside of physical laws, by and large we created the world around us. And if we made it up, we can change it.

For example, concepts like time, age, and money are constructs – we gave them their meaning so that we as human beings could have a framework in which to operate, to reduce the chaos around us.

We can choose to look at them anyway we'd like. A person who is sixty-eight can feel like he's ninety, and someone who is eighty-three can feel like she's seventeen. Some see the opportunity in five extra minutes; others think it's too short to do anything.

From the moment of our birth, major aspects of our lives were determined for us, like the country we grew up in, our family, our religion, our social circles, our education, and so much more. Our beliefs – and in turn many of our fears – are concepts that were influenced by these factors and others.

The belief systems of others and our interpretations of them created and influenced our own belief systems, our psychologies, our perceptions, our decision-making process, and our choices.

And so there are a couple of important points to mention at the outset of our journey:

First, certain choices were made for us by others on the grounds that we were helpless to make those choices ourselves. We didn't decide where we lived, where we went to school, or what religious beliefs we followed.

Second, much of our fear comes from our own imperfect interpretations of the messages we received in our environment at a young age. We couldn't imagine that something else was really bothering Mom when she exploded at us; it must have been our fault.

Third, conditions change – we grow up – giving us the opportunity and perhaps the responsibility to reinterpret what we received from others in order to become our own true selves.

In part, fear is born of that struggle between continuing to hold on to and live up to the ideals that were imprinted on us in our childhood and recreating ourselves into new, independent, and self-aware individuals.

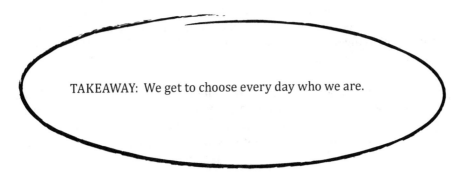

TAKEAWAY: We get to choose every day who we are.

Lesson 7

Our Nature

In symmetry with the bounty the earth provides, it is also in Her nature to deliver hurricanes, tornados, blizzards, drought, and other challenges.

~ Thich Nhat Hanh

God, grant me the serenity to accept the things I cannot change, the courage to change the things I can, and wisdom to know the difference.

~ Reinhold Niebuhr

As we go through the process in this book of creating mechanisms to overcome fear, it is useful to keep in mind two basic kinds of fear, and examine from time to time how the more potent and challenging kind of fear is impacting our lives.

First, we have a fear of *things that happen*, typically things that are beyond our control. We fear being alone. We fear growing old. We fear illness ravaging our bodies and stealing our vitality. We fear dying.

We can live in a way that will help us avoid some of these situations, but it's our nature as humans to grow old and die. This is something we can't change, but living from a place of fear and avoidance of the inevitable creates unnecessary suffering.

Second, we have a fear of *things that require our action*. This, to my mind, is a more potent and challenging fear, the kind we face on a regular basis, numerous times in a single day: meeting new people, taking exams, asking someone out on a date, interviewing for a new job, doing a home-improvement project, learning something new, dealing with stressful relationships, and countless other ways.

Day in and day out we face situations awakening our chatterbox: "I've never done this before." "This is scary." "Can I do this?" "I can't do this." "Will I succeed?" "People will see me for the fraud I am."

This kind of fear frequently shows up in our procrastination, perfectionism, control issues, and a whole range of negative emotions. Ultimately, this fear is deeply connected to what we think of ourselves, how we see our place in the world, and our concern for what others think about us.

In everything we do, it is important to try to understand "the nature of the beast" – the essence of situations awakening the fear within us. There are always two fundamental ways to do this:

First, we have to be tuned in to ourselves, who we are, what we want, why we do what we do, how we interact with the world, and so on. That can feel overwhelming, but the more we work at it, the easier and more natural it becomes.

Second, we have to be aware of others, becoming proficient at reading their signs and signals, understanding what they need, interpreting whether their reactions are actually about them instead of about us.

Being equipped with this basic understanding of fear helps us to understand what we should accept, what we can change, and what is beyond our influence, as Niebuhr suggests in the quote above. It also helps us recognize what we need to take responsibility for and what others need to own for themselves.

TAKEAWAY: We don't have to change the world, just ourselves.

Lesson 8

Awareness

Know thyself.

~ Oracle at Delphi

To find the courage within you,
give up the quest to become fearless. Concentrate
instead on being fear-conscious.

~ Sarah Quigley and Marilyn Shroyer

So many of us look outside ourselves for solutions to issues that are inside of us. We can assign blame or make excuses, but that will never change our situation. More than anything, these are efforts to protect ourselves from being vulnerable, from looking inside and facing the brutal facts (Lesson 26).

In other words, if we are expecting that our own fears will disappear as soon as those around us start behaving the way we think they should, we will be disappointed. Countless books on psychology, spirituality, inspiration, motivation, leadership, and self-improvement use the individual as the starting point and self-awareness as the foundation of all change. They show us that our issues begin and end with us.

Self-awareness is the critical ingredient without which little else is possible. We always have to work from the inside out.

Three key questions help begin the process of developing and deepening self-awareness: Who am I? What do I want? How am I going to get it?

They aren't simple questions with easy answers, but if we revisit them repeatedly over the course of our lives, the mere contemplation of them will have considerable impact on who we become.

These questions lead us to so many others, enabling us to dig deeper and deeper into self-discovery. They require us to understand where we've come from, acknowledge our current situation, and determine where we want to go.

What are we doing? Why are we doing it? Is it getting us closer to our goals? Do we even have goals? (Lesson 29)

Most importantly, asking such questions requires us to identify our fears: What are we afraid of? What has been holding us back? What are we afraid is going to happen if we let go of our fears?

We may discover that some of our fears are based on misperceptions or misunderstandings. We thought we interpreted our environment correctly. We thought we knew what the other person was thinking. It turns out our fears are frequently based on bad information.

We may come to realize that some of our fears have become ingrained like habits, like a reflex. We assume the limiting powers of our narrative are true simply because we've believed our story for so long and repeated it so often. For example, I never believed I could play music, write books, or be a professional speaker because I believed my long-standing narrative of self-pity and victimization.

The funny thing is, so many of the messages we've been interpreting in the world around us were themselves created out of fear. In essence, we have been taking in others' fears thinking we had to make them our own. It's time to break that habit.

When we increase our awareness of our fears, identify them, move toward them, and examine them, we begin to weaken them and decrease their power.

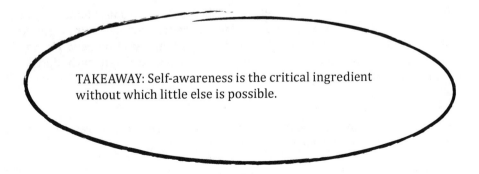

TAKEAWAY: Self-awareness is the critical ingredient without which little else is possible.

Lesson 9
Emotional Intelligence

Freedom is the will to be responsible for ourselves.

~ Friedrich Neitzsche

When we get too caught up in the busyness of the world, we lose connection with one another – and ourselves.

~ Jack Kornfield

We talk about awareness as being the critical ingredient in all change. It's important to emphasize that self-awareness is only the *starting* point. Once we refocus our thinking from being strictly outward to being primarily inward, we are just beginning to see possibilities we may not have been aware of previously.

Think about it this way. If we're holding on to anger from childhood and use it as a protective device in adulthood, we're likely not managing ourselves very well in our interactions with others.

In this case, our anger is a well-established pattern from childhood that comes out most readily when, in an instant, we re-tell ourselves our narrative of how we were wronged back then and re-enact that emotion now. We may not be aware how much this is happening, because we frequently do this subconsciously. One way to tell is to ask ourselves whether our anger is actually in proportion to the situation – whether we are overreacting.

But when we begin with ourselves, we can put in place alternate responses to anger, ones we hadn't used before, to get better outcomes.

In other words, we won't be able to get right with others until we can get right with ourselves.

Developing awareness of our emotions, managing them successfully, and using those skills to interact with others is called emotional intelligence (EI). It's difficult to hang tightly onto all of our fears and have high emotional intelligence.

The four pillars of emotional intelligence are:

1. Self-awareness
2. Self-management
3. Society awareness
4. Relationship management

Writers on EI are careful to point out that the order listed above is critical. It bears repeating: We always begin with ourselves. We may believe that others need to change in order for us to be happy. "If only my spouse didn't act that way, then I'd be happy." "If only I could get another job, then I'd be happy."

If our spouse changed or we got another job, odds are good that we'd still be unhappy.

Likewise, if we try to manage relationships having skipped the first two pillars, those relationships will likely suffer.

This may be the only time in your life someone tells you, "It's all about you," but, I'm telling you: It *is* all about you. Change comes from inside. You have to decide who you are, what you want, and how you're going to get it.

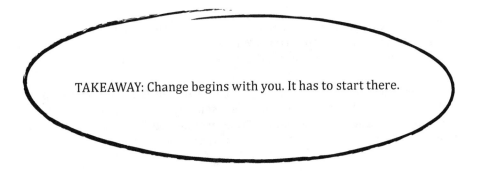

TAKEAWAY: Change begins with you. It has to start there.

Become the Chinese Farmer

All that we are is the result of what we have thought.

~ Buddha

*If you can't change the circumstances,
change your perspective.*

~ Unknown

In overcoming fear and maintaining perspective, I've found it very useful to keep in mind the story of the Chinese farmer I read in Steve Hagen's book, *Buddhism: Plain and Simple.*

One day, the only horse of a Chinese farmer runs away. The farmer's neighbor runs over and exclaims, "How terrible! Your horse ran away." The farmer responds, "Who knows what's good or bad?"

The next day the horse returns with fifty other horses trailing. The neighbor runs over and exclaims, "How wonderful! You have fifty new horses." The farmer responds, "Who knows what's good or bad?"

While breaking in one of the new horses, the farmer's son is thrown and breaks his leg. The neighbor runs over and exclaims, "How terrible! Your son broke his leg." The farmer responds, "Who knows what's good or bad?"

The next day the Chinese military comes through the town conscripting all the young males but not the farmer's son because of his broken leg. The neighbor runs over and exclaims, "How wonderful! They didn't take your son." The farmer responds, "Who knows what's good or bad?"

Where does this story end? If we're the neighbor, it never does. If we're the farmer, it just is what it is.

But don't misunderstand. "It is what it is" is not resignation to the situation. It means that we have experienced a certain situation – now, what good can we bring from it?

If we're like the neighbor, we will be shifting with the wind every time it changes direction. We will find ourselves on an emotional rollercoaster, responding to the superficial nature of events.

The farmer understands the nature of the universe and the nature of the human condition.

Most of us create our own stress, our own insecurity, our own fear, through our interpretations of what happens around us.

How we respond to this stress, insecurity, and fear will tell us a lot about how we perceive our situations.

If we are resigned to our stress, insecurity, and fear, then we perceive our situation as bad. But if we realize we do not need to feed these emotions, then we are available to look for the positivity in the situation.

Think about the power we give ourselves or deprive ourselves of based on the responses we have about the world around us.

Are we being bold and living the dream, or are we caught in the trap of constant judgment?

TAKEAWAY: Don't let your insecurities cause you to jump to negative conclusions about situations.

Lesson 11

E + R = O

*The great majority of the emotional distress
we experience results from how we think about
ourselves and our circumstances, rather than the
circumstances themselves.*

~ Thom Rutledge

*Between stimulus and response there is a space.
In that space is our power to choose our response. In
our response lies our growth and our freedom.*

~ Viktor Frankl

Much of our fear derives from our judgment of events occurring around us.

Two friends can witness the same event, but they will experience it differently. Their experience of that event is conditioned by their beliefs, their previous experiences, the environment they grew up in, their education, and a host of other factors.

In his book on fear, T.W. Walker gives a simple example. Two travelers are afraid of getting on an airplane. One person might be afraid the plane will crash, while another person might be afraid of being hijacked or kidnapped. One person's fear is based on the anxiety of dying, and the other person fears a loss of control, according to Walker.

In the same way two people can have the same fear for different reasons, several can witness or experience the same event, have different feelings about it, with some judging it as "good" and some judging it "bad."

Our *response* to events is driven by feelings, experiences, judgments – fears – that usually run deeper than the event itself. These might include anxiety about dying, fear of loss of control, fear of commitment, fear of being able to measure up, and so on.

Whether we realize it or not, we get to choose how we respond to each event that happens. Events are value neutral. They just "are." Our conditioning will influence to a large extent how we respond.

The basic equation is $E + R = O$, where E is the Event that occurs, R is our Response to the event, and O is the Outcome we are getting in our lives. What outcomes are we getting?

If we want to change the Outcomes, we just may need to change our Responses.

While there may be several or numerous factors influencing our Outcomes, it is our Response that we can change. We can't change the event. We can't change other people.

Increasing our awareness and emotional intelligence helps expand the set of responses we have in our toolkit.

In the quote above, Viktor Frankl essentially is saying we should draw out our response time to events.

When we draw out our response time, we can formulate a more thoughtful response rather than reacting instantaneously.

When we know who we are and what we want, we can make better responses and improve our outcomes.

When we improve our outcomes, we change our lives.

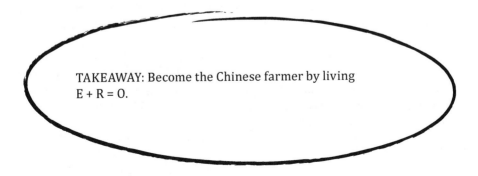

TAKEAWAY: Become the Chinese farmer by living $E + R = O$.

Lesson 12

Belief and Fear

The best things in life are unexpected, because there were no expectations.

~ Eli Khamarov

The outer conditions of a person's life will always be found to reflect their inner beliefs.

~ James Allen

What is it we believe about ourselves and the world around us?

That's what a lot of fear issues come down to: our beliefs. Many of us live with expectations about ourselves and our beliefs about others' expectations of us. Fear is frequently generated by the gap between these expectations and "reality."

I had two very powerful beliefs among the many that kept me imprisoned by fear.

The first was I had to be perfect. I'm not even sure I could say what "perfect" would have looked like, but it was a very powerful thought. Straight As? Always obedient? Never a problem for my parents? The cleverest person in the room?

Of course, I wasn't any of those things. The gap between those expectations and reality fueled my fear and, in turn, paralyzed me in my tracks. I had a head full of things I wanted to do, things I thought would be fun and exciting, but I hardly did any of them (until much later in life) because of my belief that I would never be good enough at them. I wouldn't be perfect.

The second belief was I needed to be accepted and validated by people around me in order to be worthy as a human being. As the ninth of twelve kids, growing up I was constantly trying to get validation from everyone in the family.

I constantly compared my insides to others' outsides. I decided they must have been super confident and without fear, based on their accomplishments. I convinced myself I could never be as good as them. I could never do what they could do. I would never be acceptable.

When we think about our beliefs and fears, it's useful to explore why we do what we do.

Do we buy expensive cars and clothing because we can afford them and want to treat ourselves or do we believe they will draw positive attention to us and give us value?

Do we gossip about or make fun of others because we believe it makes us feel superior and gives us a sense of self-worth and acceptability?

Do we believe we need to be accepted by everyone in order to be acceptable?

In many ways, the dilemma is fairly straightforward:

If our belief, our sense of self, is built on being the smartest in the room and someone smarter walks in, what happens to us?

If we believe we have to be the best looking in the room and someone more attractive walks in, what happens to us?

If we believe that our self-worth and confidence are based on others' opinions, and they don't like us, what happens to us?

TAKEAWAY: What do you believe about yourself and how is it linked to your fear?

Taking Action to Create Belief

*As you work to overcome your self-created
limitations, talk to your subconscious, telling it that
instead of reacting, you're now going to respond
with conscious choices.*

~ Wayne Dyer

*You gain strength, courage, and confidence by
every experience in which you really stop to look
fear in the face.... You must do the thing
you think you cannot do.*

~ Eleanor Roosevelt

It's critical to understand that, ultimately, our biggest obstacles are our self-limiting beliefs.

This may be the single most important idea to grapple with as we imagine the kind of life we want. It's frequently the only thing standing between us and success.

Success isn't really about knowing how to do something. Everything we need is already inside of us and everything we need to know is out there waiting for us to pick it up.

We know how to lose weight. We know how to get good grades in school. We know how to become a millionaire. We even know how to land on Mars. And, yes, we know how to overcome fear.

Do we *believe* we can do it?

A question like this can be a tremendous burden. Most of us can't change our perspective simply by thinking about it. Reflection and contemplation are necessary, but it's frequently not enough when we're trying to prove to ourselves "We can!"

I have found a great way to create positive belief is to act. Pick a relatively small task, like cleaning out a junk drawer or walking a quarter of a mile. Just pick one thing, focus on it, and do it. There, you've done it. You've proven to yourself it's possible.

Acting and believing go hand in hand. The more we act, the more we believe. The more we believe, the more we can act in the face of fear. We start to get excited about what's possible and we want more of it. We start to do what's possible. After a while, we start to do what we thought impossible.

As we realize the possibilities for our own lives, we will stop inviting negative, toxic people in. We will decrease our gossip, our criticism of other people, and the excuses we rely on to stay safe.

After a while, we will start to see patterns and realize we do everything the same way. Reducing fear and going after what we want will become easier.

I saw these patterns when I studied Russian, Chinese, and Spanish, when I wrote books, when I learned to play music, when I tackled public speaking, when I worked with the media, and everything else I've done. Once I learned how to do one, I knew how to tackle the next, and it got easier and easier.

And this from a guy who believed nothing was possible.

Once we truly believe that our biggest obstacle is the way we look at ourselves and our situations, our ability to do something about it will improve dramatically.

TAKEAWAY: Everything we need is already here. It's time to create our belief in ourselves.

Acceptance

Accept your past without regret, handle your present with confidence, and face your future without fear.

~ Unknown

I now see how owning our story and loving ourselves through that process is the bravest thing that we will ever do.

~ Brené Brown

Like all people, we want to be heard, we want to be respected, and we want to be loved. We want to feel like we belong. We don't want to be driven out of the tribe – whether that's family, friends, colleagues, or any other group.

A lot of our fear seems to be based on the worry of losing that connection. If we don't measure up, we will be invited to leave, lose our identity, be alone, and perhaps be without a means of survival.

Think about the things we are most afraid of and trace them back to this idea.

We're afraid of making a mistake, embarrassing ourselves, being criticized, failing, and a lot more. We want to please those around us for fear they won't accept us.

Think about it in your own lives. What are you afraid of? What are your worst case scenarios?

Am I attractive enough (for other people)? Am I smart enough (for other people)? Am I successful enough (for other people)? Am I funny enough (for other people)? Have I made my parents proud? Will my spouse still love me if I speak my mind? Will people laugh at me?

The chatterbox in our heads repeats messages we've interpreted over the years, reminding us that we have to be acceptable and accepted.

"I have to please my parents." "What will people think of me?" "I want it to be perfect, otherwise...." "My worth is equal to my performance. If I don't perform well enough...." "What if it's not good enough?" "What if....?" "What if....?" "What if....?"

Our chatterbox frequently serves to undermine us even though we may think it's protecting us from harm. In many cases, it's protecting us from getting outside our comfort zone.

But, *outside* the comfort zone is where everything happens: challenges, struggle, adversity, mistakes, growth, understanding, insight, courage, success, and joy.

One important part we'll discuss throughout the book is being aware of whose acceptance we are trying to earn. Who is it we're trying to impress? Why are we trying to be accepted by them? What are *they* afraid of? What is their motivation to get me to act a certain way? What would really happen if I don't impress them? What will happen if I fail?

Are those others locked down in fear or are they fulfilling their goals and going after their dreams?

TAKEAWAY: We don't have to be accepted by everyone else to be enough. Being exactly who we are is what matters.

Excuses and the Blame Game

When we can no longer change a situation, we are challenged to change ourselves.

~ Viktor Frankl

I don't run away from a challenge because I am afraid. Instead, I run toward it because the only way to escape fear is to trample it beneath your feet.

~ Nadia Comaneci

Why is it some can achieve everything they want and others don't? Both groups have the same amount of time available to them. And they both have access to excuses. What makes them different?

The answer lies in what they choose to focus on.

We can use the blame game as a convenient and comfortable way to avoid fear and to spend our time criticizing others. That way, we don't have to face our own shortcomings and take responsibility for the position we're in. Ironically, searching for excuses, blaming everyone but ourselves, and being excessively critical of those around us are the expressions of our own underlying fear.

Unfortunately, this way of being also keeps us from moving forward, from accomplishing what we need to, and from being successful in life.

The blame game can take many forms. We typically use excuses as a way of fostering self-limiting beliefs while blaming everything and everyone but ourselves. Excuses are essentially a way for us to quit before we even start.

But it will be difficult.

But it will take a long time.

But there will be family drama.

But I don't deserve it.

But I can't afford it.

But no one will help me.

But it has never been done.

But I'm not smart enough.

But I don't have the time.

But I don't have the energy.

The list goes on and on.

Attitude distinguishes those who rely on excuses from those who don't. We always have the power to choose.

We can choose to blame our parents for our lack of progress. We can choose to blame our lack of resources. We can choose to blame an illness or handicap. Or we can choose to be happy. We can choose to adopt a positive attitude. We can find the resources. We can choose to fight for the life we want.

Successful people don't look for excuses. They understand blaming everyone else is a trap: It doesn't get them closer to their goals and it fills their heart with negativity and defeat.

TAKEAWAY: Let's get off our "buts" and take charge of our destiny.

Stop Killing Time

Almost all worry evolves from the conflict between intuition and inaction.

~ Gavin De Becker

Among the aimless you often hear talk about killing time. People who are constantly killing time are really killing their own chances in life.
Those who are destined to become successful are those who make time and use it wisely.

~ Arthur Brisbane

Procrastination is one of the methods we use in psychological warfare with ourselves when we're trapped in a battle with perfectionism.

For me, procrastination was a means of survival, or at least that's how it played in my mind.

When I was growing up, my father was the most influential authority figure in my life. He was bright, educated, charming, and savvy to the ways of the world. He worked hard and was an amazing provider for our family of fourteen.

Along with that came a philosophy that praise was not necessary for a child who was doing what was expected. Only when some extraordinary achievement was reached would there be acknowledgment, and that turned out to be a thumbs-up from across the room.

Over the years, I came to realize that many of his fellow immigrants and others of his generation had a similar philosophy. I'm sure part it was the burning need to see their children survive in a tough world. After all, that generation had suffered hardships we would never know, and they needed to keep up the pressure on us to succeed.

Perhaps all would have been lost for me had I not caught my father bragging about his kids to outsiders. He was proud, but it seems he chose not to let that secret known to us in order to protect us from resting on our laurels.

Without my father's acknowledgement and praise, the message I interpreted was that nothing I did would ever be good enough. But here's the point: He never actually said, "You're not good enough." My interpretation of his messages pushed me right into the arms of procrastination.

For me, procrastination became a savior of sorts. On the one side, mistakes felt like they were punished. On the other side, an excellent performance carried no upside. I was scared of how hard something would be, so I didn't dive into it. I was afraid of failing at it, so I put it off. Putting things off meant I could justify my performance with lies to myself like, "I did what I could." "If I only had more time...." "Well, it would have been better if...." You know the drill.

But procrastination isn't that simple. I wasn't just protecting myself. I was still hungry for the approval. I still believed that my self-worth was tied to my performance. I ended up paralyzed instead of taking action.

In reality, my procrastination served to *reinforce* the belief that I wasn't good enough – and this had nothing to do with my father. I convinced myself that I couldn't and so I didn't. I wasn't allowing myself to become myself.

To my mind, it isn't only the case that procrastination is driven by fear. It seems that the procrastination itself reinforces the fear. The time-wasting, the wringing of hands, and the failure to act in a healthy way convince us time and again that there is something to fear.

TAKEAWAY: Procrastination is the vicious practice of keeping ourselves from becoming ourselves.

Lesson 17

Embracing Imperfection

Striving for excellence motivates you; striving for perfection is demoralizing.

~ Harriet Braiker

Ring the bells that still can ring
Forget your perfect offering.
There is a crack in everything.
That's how the light gets in.

~ Leonard Cohen

For many of us, perfectionism plays a major role in our lives. As a recovering perfectionist, I know it influenced the vast majority of my thoughts and actions for years.

My "emotional logic" was if only I could be perfect, I would be good enough, I would measure up, and I would be acceptable to the people who mattered most.

I operated under a lot of faulty beliefs.

I believed being perfect was a single occurrence, that there was an end point; once I was perfect then everything would be OK. But I learned the quest for perfection is never finished, even if others do recognize us. It is a constant campaign for validation.

I believed making mistakes and experiencing failure were signs of weakness and an indictment of me as a person. I believed perfectionism and excellence were the same things. *I have come to realize that mistakes and failure – and getting up again – are the keys to success.*

I believed there was one right way, and that right way was the one held by the people I was trying to impress. If they disagreed with my approach, and they were smarter, more experienced, or wealthier than me, then they must be right and I was wrong. In other words, not perfect.

I believed other people had their act together. I didn't understand they might have been fighting their own battles with perfectionism. I didn't understand they were probably struggling for their own validation. My overriding belief was that they were better than me.

I believed everyone had to agree with me and everyone had to like me. In order for that to happen, I had to be perfect in everyone's eyes. In the throes of perfectionism, it's difficult to see the irrationality of this belief.

I believed through perfect accomplishments I could make myself worthy of love.

The sin of perfectionism is it frequently results in procrastination. The sin of perfectionism is we discount our efforts, our achievements – our lives – because of our failure to reach a standard that's impossible to meet.

It's important to keep one simple fact in mind: Perfection is unattainable.

What may resonate with me may not resonate with others. Someone will disagree with our point of view or dislike our performance. And that's natural.

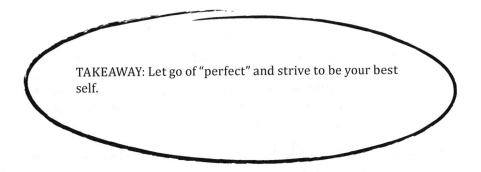

TAKEAWAY: Let go of "perfect" and strive to be your best self.

Others Care Far Less Than You Think

*Enjoy your own life without comparing it with
that of another.*

~ Marquis de Condorcet

*You may not control all the events that happen to
you, but you can decide not to be reduced by them.*

~ Maya Angelou

We spend countless hours worrying what others are going to think about us. In essence, we give our power and energy away. We make our lives about their opinions, assessments, criticisms, and judgments of us.

Of course, we want to be acceptable and accepted. We don't want to be alone.

There are a couple of basic points we should keep in mind:

First, we need to bear in mind the words of Ricky Nelson's song, "Garden Party": "You see, you can't please everybody so you got to please yourself." The simple mathematics of it is we can't please *everyone*. And we don't necessarily even need to please everyone in our circle. When we strip it down, the number of people we *have to please* is very small: one, ourselves.

What we do need are healthy relationships based on mutual respect, concern, consideration, and support.

Second, when we're in the throes of our fear, whether expressed as perfectionism, procrastination, or any of the other myriad ways, we easily forget that those people we're trying to impress are struggling with fears of their own. They may even be trying to get acceptance from us and we don't know it.

We spend so much time posing and posturing, worrying and agonizing, in order to get acceptance from others. It's time we tried that hard to be accepted by ourselves.

Third, others simply care far less about what's going on in our lives than we think. They think about us far less than we think they do. I spent countless hours worrying about what people thought of me, trying to manipulate situations to create a favorable response to make me feel good.

I hung on to things they said that struck a nerve – that hurt my feelings – for years, agonizing over them and letting them define me. Of course, the people who said those things forgot all about it two minutes after it happened, if they even ever realized it happened.

It's not that they were nasty, mean, or callous.

Part of it was, in my state of super sensitivity and being locked down in fear, I brought far more meaning to others' words than they themselves brought to their own words.

Part of it was that people simply have other things to do. They have other things on their minds than us – like themselves.

Nothing we do will ever be as important to them as it is to us.

Nothing we do will ever be as important to them as their own issues, concerns, and lives.

TAKEAWAY: Don't try to give your power away to others. They actually don't want it.

Lesson 19
Choose Your Responses

*You don't have to attend every argument
you're invited to.*

~ Unknown

*To be addicted to control is to be
endlessly out of control.*

~ Thom Rutledge

Many times our fear, our need to protect ourselves, or our narrative from the past dictates or drives the responses we make.

When we choose our responses, we have an option to have an extreme negative response, an extreme positive response, or anything in between.

Once, at a conference I was hosting, a woman stood up and took me to task in front of the audience of 150 women. Years later, when I was delivering a program on overcoming fear, I told the participants the story about the conference and asked for examples of an extreme negative response I could have given to the woman.

One person said, "Sit your ass down." Of course the participants laughed. And, yes, I could have said that.

But what would I have gained? For a few seconds I might have felt good about putting that woman "in her place." After that it would have been all downhill. At least some, if not many, in the audience would have been upset. Someone likely would have called my boss. I would have paid for that remark for days and possibly weeks or months thereafter.

More importantly, had I given a response like that, I know it would have been driven by fear. I would have gone into self-protect mode, felt embarrassed, and tried to get my revenge. There is nothing productive about a response like that.

There was no negative fallout from that experience because I chose the extreme positive response. "Thank you so much for your input. I appreciate that. I'll look into it immediately."

When someone starts yelling at us, we have a choice to make. Of course, it's not a pleasant experience, and often we choose to yell back. Our thinking might be something like, "That person made me so mad!"

As we consider our responses, we can ask ourselves questions like, "Is that person's response really about the issue or about his or her fear?" "Does the fact that this person has chosen to yell mean that I, too, have to yell?"

The fact of the matter is no one forces us to argue. We choose. We choose to engage. We choose to raise our voice. We choose to believe everything is about us. We choose to believe that everything requires a response. We choose to believe that people have so much power over us.

The right response, for me, is the one that is not based in fear, and serves both me and the other person involved whenever possible.

TAKEAWAY: Choose responses that are aligned with your dreams, not your fears.

Successful People's View on Fear

A man's errors are his portals of discovery.

~ James Joyce

Of course there is no formula for success except, perhaps, an unconditional acceptance of life and what it brings.

~ Arthur Rubinstein

We're not going to wish our fears away, and we can't wish our dreams into being.

We try, of course.

Just look at the amount of money spent on lottery tickets or on pills designed to change us without us having to do the work.

But that's not reality, that's wishful thinking. The last thing we want to do is look closely at ourselves – at our fear – for fear of what we might find. The beliefs we've created about ourselves can be terrifying, even if they're not true. Many of us have already long ago convinced ourselves that "we can't handle it."

To paraphrase Henry Ford: If you think you can, you're right. If you think you can't, you're right.

I've always been interested in how successful people think and act and how those differ from the way the rest of us do things. I think one of the keys is how successful people handle their fear.

When I refer to "successful" people, I'm not talking about those who are wealthy, but as a result of handling their fear, many have become affluent. I'm not talking about people with perfect relationships, but they understand how to build meaningful relationships. I'm not talking about workaholics and "power brokers." Successful people maintain balance and perspective among work, play, family, friends, hobbies, finances, health, vices, and other aspects of their lives.

Successful people seem to have a very even, high-performing Wheel of Life (Lesson 27).

Some things I've observed about successful people:

- They don't publicly dwell on and beat themselves up over "mistakes." They understand that mistakes are really opportunities in disguise. They try to learn the lesson and move on.
- They don't spend time gossiping or sticking their noses in other people's business.
- They have worked on the answers to these questions: Who am I? What do I want? How am I going to get it? It's easy to see they've worked on them by the way they live their lives.
- They don't panic at the first signs of adversity or if something doesn't go according to plan. They ask questions, assess the situation, remain flexible, weigh their options, and move on.

As we can easily see, these are not the habits of people who are led by fear.

Perhaps the most effective tools successful people have in their toolkit are the mechanisms they use to stay on track (Lesson 22). With the right mechanisms in place, they push through the fear rather than wallow in it.

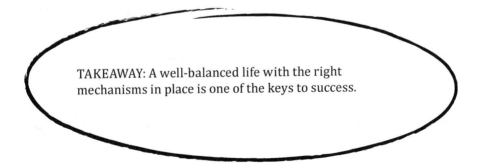

TAKEAWAY: A well-balanced life with the right mechanisms in place is one of the keys to success.

Process

*Live as if you were to die tomorrow. Learn as if you
were to live forever.*

~ Mahatma Gandhi

*Do not wait until the conditions are perfect to begin.
Beginning makes the conditions perfect.*

~ Alan Cohen

We know that without a specific goal we will not be nearly as efficient and effective as we could be. We won't have a good sense of exactly where we're going.

We also need to understand, while the goal is critical, the journey – the process – is central to getting us to the goal. Focusing exclusively on the goal means we may not be giving the process enough attention. The goal alone may prove so grandiose it activates our fear, and we're defeated even before we start. We may miss the process if we're fixated on the goal.

The process is where we live for the duration of going after the goal. When we manage the process, we manage fear.

The rest of this book deals primarily with issues of process. The point I'd like to make here regards the mindset we have as we go through the process. Are we perfectionists or optimalists?

I love Tal Ben-Shahar's contrast of perfectionists and optimalists in his book, *The Pursuit of Perfect*. These two types of people hold views of the process that are very different.

Perfectionists see the journey as a straight line with no obstacles, no distractions, and no detours. They focus primarily or solely on the destination using all-or-nothing thinking. Perfectionists are frequently defensive, harsh, rigid, and static, expert fault finders who are hyper-critical.

Optimists expect to find deviations, twists, and turns on the path. The line to success is an irregular spiral – squiggly and messy. Failure is feedback rather than indictment. Optimists focus on both the journey and the destination. Their thinking is complex and nuanced as they remain flexible, adaptable, dynamic, and open to suggestions. Optimists are forgiving of self and others.

In my days as a perfectionist, I would consider a goal and, even before I got started, identify all of the difficulties and imagine them as insurmountable. I was looking for the straight line with no obstacles. I was essentially looking for reasons to fail.

If I started a project and anyone made a critical comment, I would begin to crumble. If anything seemed difficult or I felt I wasn't smart enough to solve it, I became instantly frustrated. Everything happened in my mind, and I was defeated instantly. If it wasn't going to be perfect then it wasn't going to be at all.

I missed out on a lot of wonderful parts of the process. I missed the joy of discovery. I missed the satisfaction of working through difficult issues. I missed giving myself over totally to a task. Fear was always lurking.

When we have a process in place, the only thing we have to worry about is what we do today. Yesterday's gone and tomorrow hasn't arrived yet. If we had a bad day yesterday executing our process, we don't have to carry it over to today. Let's be clear with ourselves: We *choose* to carry it over – we make that decision to focus on what went wrong yesterday.

TAKEAWAY: There is no right way to achieve your goal. Work your process and stay flexible to new opportunities.

Mechanisms

Continuous effort – not strength or intelligence – is the key to unlocking our potential.

~ Winston Churchill

Success will never be a big step in the future; success is a small step taken just now.

~ Jonatan Mårtensson

In Lesson 20, I mentioned that successful people have the right mechanisms in place to help them get what they want. In this book, we're talking about mechanisms for minimizing fear.

I prefer the word "mechanism" because it indicates a system of parts working together. If we think about a machine, the mechanism is critical to making it function. And it functions smoothly because the right parts are in the right places, integrated, and they undergo regular maintenance.

We need the right mechanisms in our lives to help us deal with fear.

Successful people define who they are, what they want, and how they're going to get it. They know fear will raise its head along the way, but they don't let it stop them from defining their dreams and setting their goals.

As they go forward, they put countless mechanisms in place to ensure their success, such as exercises, electronic tools, habits, support from others, and so on. Some of the mechanisms include:

- Deciding. Committing. Succeeding. (Lesson 23)
- Thinking in advance (Lesson 24)
- Creating a Wheel of Life (Lesson 27)
- Doing a SWOT analysis (Lesson 28)
- Rewriting their personal narratives (Lesson 31)
- Breaking down complex tasks (Lesson 38)

These are all mechanisms successful people use to address issues of fear, stay on track with their goals, and maintain perspective.

Without mechanisms it becomes far more difficult, if not impossible, to successfully maneuver through fear when it arises. The result can be psychological paralysis and months or years of wasted time.

Indeed, the purpose of having mechanisms is to temper the impact of fear.

The mechanisms are successful because they prescribe action that is very practical, very specific, and results-oriented.

As psychotherapist Thom Rutledge points out in his book, *Embracing Fear*, successful people change their conversation with the Bully, the voice of neurotic fear.

Instead of agreeing with the Bully in order to protect themselves from the possibility of failure, they look the Bully squarely in the eye and say, "Okay, you have my full attention. Tell me again about all the bad stuff that is going to happen to me if I don't listen to you. Be sure to make it sound real scary."

TAKEAWAY: Mechanisms help successful people be bold and live the dream.

Part 2

Assessment Mechanisms

Decide, Commit, Succeed

Do or do not. There is no try.

~ Yoda

Until one is committed, there is hesitancy, the chance to draw back. Whatever you can do or dream you can, begin it. Boldness has genius, power, and magic in it. Begin it now.

~ Johann Wolfgang von Goethe

Fear is frequently generated by uncertainty – uncertainty about what we want, uncertainty about how to get it, uncertainty surrounding our ability to get it, and uncertainty about others' opinions about us.

We often dream about things we want, expressing a desire to live a better life, to have more money, to improve our relationships, and so on. But far more rarely do we use mechanisms to clarify exactly what we want and how we're going to get it.

As a recovering procrastinator, I've watched countless hours of television. I remember the early days of commercials for P90X, the extreme exercise workout regimen, when they could be seen only at two or three o'clock in the morning.

The thing that caught my eye, besides the madness of the workout itself, was the motto of Beach Body, the parent company of P90X: Decide. Commit. Succeed.

This is one of the easiest mechanisms to memorize and carry with us at all times. Decide. Commit. Succeed.

Here's a keystone question to ask ourselves: "Have I decided what I want?"

Don't take this word "decided" too lightly. We either decide or we don't decide; there is no in-between. Unfortunately, many times we "decide" several times a week: I'm going to do this. No, I'm going to do that. I've changed my mind; I'm going to do something else. That's not deciding.

Either we've decided or we haven't. We can't have it both ways.

Deciding is critically important...but it's not enough. Here's what I mean.

Five frogs are sitting on a log. One decides to jump off. How many frogs remain on the log? The answer, of course, is five. The frog that decided to jump, did just that....decided. He didn't actually jump. We can decide all we want, but until we act – with a plan in hand – our decisions don't mean much.

Once we've decided we want to be in charge of our lives, that we want to deal with our fear, we ask ourselves: "Are we committed to it?" We're either truly committed or we're not.

Let's not fool ourselves. We can't be committed to an undertaking and not committed at the same time.

For me, a commitment in this sense is not simply a promise that we are going to do something. It is the action. We display our commitment day-in and day-out in the doing of a thing. True commitment is staying with the program even when it is inconvenient or difficult.

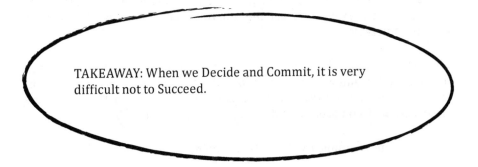

TAKEAWAY: When we Decide and Commit, it is very difficult not to Succeed.

Think in Advance

Worry is not preparation.

~ Cheri Huber

You can't solve a problem with the same mind that created it.

~ Albert Einstein

I often think about boot camps and training academies – the kinds of places where "thinking in advance" is taught to attendees.

Institutions like that are set up to provide as much training as possible so when their personnel find themselves in difficult situations, they have a mindset for resolving them. They have been put through a wide variety of scenarios, and have had the core principles of their organizations instilled in them.

It doesn't do anyone any good to start to learn how to solve a problem the moment it arises. Thinking in advance reduces uncertainty and fear, and it keeps us poised to respond when the situation and our emotions become fluid and unpredictable.

Thinking in advance helps us decide what we stand for, what we are willing to compromise, and what we won't tolerate. The more scenarios we imagine and decisions we make in advance, the easier it will be to face them when they arise, with focus on process and outcome rather than on fear.

Here's a simple example to illustrate this point:

Step 1: Acknowledge the context. You and your spouse grew up in households where there was a lot of yelling. Both of you know how it feels to live in an environment like that and don't want it. You are both aware of the idea of Decide, Commit, Succeed.

Step 2: Decide. Both of you decide you don't want any yelling in your house. This is a great step, but it's not enough. There's no mechanism in place yet to strengthen your resolve.

Step 3: Commit. This is the important part. Commit to each other that there won't be yelling in the house *by not yelling*. Real commitment shows up in our actions. You both commit by creating alternative responses (E + R = 0) to yelling, like asking for a few minutes to get your thoughts together. When the telltale signs of anger, stress, impatience, and frustration start to show themselves, you can now rely on effective mechanisms that are already in place.

Step 4: Succeed. When you choose an alternative response in advance, it opens the possibility to create a totally different environment. When there is no yelling, there is more peace, which increases the probability of dialogue. When there's constructive dialogue and peaceful resolution of differences, there is less need to activate the intense fear that accompanies protecting our egos.

The first couple of times we use thinking in advance to its logical and fullest conclusion, as outlined above, something shifts. We realize there are alternatives. Relationships change. Fear lessens. Life improves.

Thinking in advance can be used in virtually every aspect of our lives, from what time we get up in the morning to the jobs we take to the lives we lead.

But it's difficult to think in advance if you don't know what you want. Fear can't conquer the person who knows his heart and mind.

TAKEAWAY: Thinking ahead about your responses leads to new possibilities for better outcomes and a happier life.

Lesson 25

Determine What You Want

Set peace of mind as your highest goal, and organize your life around it.

~ Brian Tracy

No valid plans for the future can be made by those who have no capacity for living now.

~ Alan Watts

We've started discussing some of the assessment mechanisms we can use to reduce our fear, like deciding, committing, and thinking in advance. Determining what we want is one of the most important mechanisms in this system we're building.

Without a goal, destination, or final objective, we'll find ourselves running aimlessly or stalled out. We will end up somewhere, but it may not be a place we want to be.

Many of us don't take the time to really decide what we want, partly because of the fear attached to uncertainty or what others would think about us.

The key to the next mechanism, Determine What You Want, is asking some basic questions of ourselves to assess where we are, what we like, and where we might want to go.

- What is the thing I look forward to more than anything?
- What am I doing when time flies?
- In what capacity do I want to have these activities in my life? As hobbies? As full-time paid employment?

- What are my skills?
- Where is the intersection between what I'm good at and what I'm passionate about?
- Would other people with my skills agree that I'm good at them?
- Do I need further education to pursue the thing I'm passionate about?
- Do I like working with people or technology?
- Do I want to work in an office or at home?
- Do I want to work indoors or outdoors?
- Do I want to work a traditional eight to five job?
- How many hours a day do I want to work?
- How many days a week do I want to work?
- How much money do I need to make per year to maintain my lifestyle?
- How much money would I like to make per year?
- What are my family's needs?
- To what extent are their requirements informing my decision?
- How will it benefit my kids if I make a change (e.g., showing them the importance of going after their dreams)?
- Is there a line of work I would be passionate about that could include my family in some way?

For a wonderful exploration of questions we can ask for our life journey, check out *What Would a Wise Woman Do? Questions to Ask Along the Way*, by Laura Atchison, a #1 bestseller on Amazon.com. Don't let the title scare you away, men; it's great for you as well.

TAKEAWAY: The questions we ask along the way – and the responses to these questions – influence where we end up.

Lesson 26
Face the Brutal Facts

Every time I've had a bad performance at an event, I've come back more determined and focused.

~ Shaun White

Courage – the quality of daring to crawl out from under the covers to respond to fear with fresh attention and appropriate responses.

~ Sarah Quigley

It's easy to give in to fear and not act.

If we don't act, we say to ourselves, we can spare ourselves the anxiety of having to face a less-than-perfect self.

If we do act, and it doesn't go well, we're forced to acknowledge we're not perfect and risk shame, guilt, and other uncomfortable emotions.

But once we choose to realize that perfection, procrastination, and blaming are no-win situations, we can move forward.

In his book, *Good to Great*, author Jim Collins discusses the attributes of great companies, one of which is the ability to "face the brutal facts," as he calls it. Only by objectively assessing performance and being willing to make adjustments did these companies excel.

And, of course, this doesn't apply just to companies.

One way to rein in fear and improve any aspect of our lives is to muster up the courage to look at our shortcomings in the cold light of day.

Don't take this lightly. Performance assessment is critical to success. And, when we think about it, honest, continual review is a no-lose proposition.

We can congratulate ourselves for what went well – celebrating the small wins – and we can identify necessary changes for improvement. Over time, we will recognize our progress.

The more we move through all aspects of our lives with a review mechanism in place, the less intimidating fear will become.

Think about the rock group, U2. After every concert they meet with their manager to talk about what went well and what needs work.

The U.S. Navy precision flying team, the Blue Angels, does the same. After a performance, the pilots assemble to analyze the flight, reinforce what went well, and discuss what could be done better.

It's not a coincidence that U2 and the Blue Angels are considered among the best in the world in their fields.

We get the nerve to face the facts about all aspects of our lives by reflecting on them, making notes on them, and getting feedback from people we trust.

A great place to start is by doing a simple, one-minute exercise called the Wheel of Life (Lesson 27).

Face the facts. Commit to making steady improvement. You will be changing your relationship with fear before you know it.

TAKEAWAY: Honestly evaluating your life will get you further than blame and procrastination.

The Wheel of Life

Make the most of yourself,
because that's all there is of you.

~ Ralph Waldo Emerson

I have done my best. That is all the philosophy of
living one needs.

~ Lin-yutang

Facing the facts can be a confusing, traumatic experience filled with an overwhelming amount of information and delicate, uncomfortable realities.

You may think things like: Where do I start? How can I look at everything in my life? It hurts too much to look that closely at myself. I'm ok; I don't have to fix anything.

In my programs, I use a very simple exercise to help people get a quick, but impactful, visual depiction of their lives in less than a minute. I'm going to teach you how do that exercise yourself.

Draw a circle with eight segments in it, like a pizza pie cut in eight slices. Each slice should have a label at the end, on the outside curve of the slice.

Label the eight sections: health, family and friends, romance, personal growth, fun and recreation, physical environment, business/career, and finances.

Inside each slice, create a scale ranging from one at the center point of the pie to ten at the outer edge. Then, simply circle the number that best represents where you are in your life today.

For example, if your relationships with your family and friends are great, circle number nine or ten. If your health is just so-so, circle number five. If your finances are in the pits, circle number one.

After you have graded each of the eight categories, reflecting how you think you're doing in life, connect each number you've circled to the next with a line, going around the pizza. In this way, you are connecting the marks and making your own wheel of your own life.

If things are really strong in each area of your life, your marks will all be up in the eight-to-ten range.

Most of us, however, have one or several areas where things just aren't quite up to par.

We're in debt and doing nothing to fix it. Our eating and sleeping habits are such that we're unhealthy and frequently sick. We work too much, and don't take time for fun and recreation. Here, our marks are typically below five.

When there are several categories with low marks, our wheel hardly resembles a circle. We're trying to run our life on a bumpy tire.

The most important part of the exercise is to reflect on the categories with the low marks and understanding what role fear is playing in each of those categories.

Are we afraid to face something about ourselves? The shape of the wheel is typically a reflection of our inner life.

TAKEAWAY: Assessing the state of your life is a great step toward understanding your weaknesses so you can make improvements.

Lesson 28

Analyze Your SWOT

The unexamined life is not worth living.

~ Socrates

Our greatness lies not so much in being able to remake the world as being able to remake ourselves.

~ Mahatma Gandhi

SWOT is an acronym used in business circles; companies frequently perform SWOT analyses on projects, deals, or business ventures. SWOT stands for Strengths, Weaknesses, Opportunities, and Threats.

As with many other business concepts, SWOT can be applied to our personal lives as a mechanism to counter fear.

I think of a SWOT analysis as the next level down from the Wheel of Life in the assessment of our situations.

The key, as with the Wheel of Life, is to do an honest assessment of our lives. Face the brutal facts.

Doing this in the context of other mechanisms can be a particularly useful exercise as we will be able to see how our SWOT interacts with our E + R = O to influence our Wheel of Life.

For example, if we're bad at saying no to people when they ask for our time, this may be a weakness of ours (SWOT). One of the Outcomes (E + R = O) from that lack of discipline in our Response may be constant arguments with loved ones because we over-commit and don't follow through. We may notice that our relationships with friends and family aren't so great (Wheel of Life).

If you want a challenging exercise, list five strengths and five weaknesses you have. (Yes, it's important to write them down.) Most people can list two or three of each quickly and then they get stuck. Make your list now, before you continue reading.

Are you clear about your strengths and weaknesses?

Are your strengths greater than you expected? Frequently we suffer from fear and its various symptoms (procrastination, perfectionism, anxiety, etc.), getting lost inside our own minds and forgetting the vast opportunities that surround us.

What are the threats in your environment that keep you from capitalizing on your strengths and mobilizing your resources?

Are you attuned to opportunities around you? Do you spend time building relationships that can create more opportunities?

What weaknesses do you have that may be holding you back? Are you giving them too much attention?

The analysis can help identify where our passions may lie, bring greater focus to the direction we want our lives to take, and address some of the potential obstacles we may meet along the way.

When we assess our situation, we can see clearly. When we see clearly, it becomes easier to act. When we act, we gain experience. When we gain experience, our confidence increases. When our confidence increases, we can put our fear into perspective.

TAKEAWAY: Clarity about our positives and negatives helps drive down fear.

Lesson 29

Get SMART

*Setting goals is the first step in turning the
invisible into the visible.*

~ Tony Robbins

*What you get by achieving your goals
is not as important as what you become by
achieving your goals.*

~ Johann von Goethe

Goal setting may come as a surprise in a book on fear, but it is a critical mechanism in the process of challenging our fears.

Fear gets a lot of its energy and momentum from uncertainty and a lack of clarity. After all, if we don't know where we're headed, we end up going where life takes us, which probably isn't where we want to go. So we need a plan.

That plan is supported when we explore questions like who am I, what do I want, and how am I going to get it. When we do a good job addressing those questions, our direction is determined and the path ahead seems a bit clearer.

Goal setting forces us to get very practical, very specific, and very action-oriented. It requires we get very real.

A very simple mechanism we can use to help drive down our fear is a SMART goal. SMART goals are the difference between wishful thinking and making real progress.

S – Specific. Our goal has to be as specific as possible while being flexible to unforeseen factors. "I want to lose weight" is not a goal. There's a lot of room for fear to enter. "I am going to lose fifteen pounds between January 1st and February 15th, and here's how I'm going to do it" is a much more specific goal, making it more difficult for fear to throw us off target.

M – Measurable. We have to know what it is exactly we are trying to do. How will we know when we've reached the goal? What does "done" look like? In our weight-loss example, it's fifteen pounds.

A – Attainable. Is it actually possible to reach this goal? Losing 100 pounds in a week is not a realistic, but losing fifteen in six weeks is within reach.

R – Results-oriented. We set goals like we set a destination when we get in the car – with the expectation we will get there. The pursuit of goals is critical, but we can't forget that we actually need to arrive at our destination.

T – Time-bound. In our weight-loss example above, we set a time limit of six weeks. Deadlines are important when trying to reach a goal. When we commit to meeting them, we minimize the time we have to think about fear.

I'm a big fan of adding two letters at the end to make our goals SMARTER.

E – Evaluate and R – Re-evaluate. Assessing the actions we took and progress made is a crucial part of reaching goals. It identifies what we didn't think about before we set out. We can see why something didn't work as we expected. We can learn what we need to improve next time.

By the way, for the longest time I believed I couldn't lose weight. Fear played a central role in that. When I got SMARTER and created a real goal, I did, in fact, lose fifteen pounds in six weeks. And another ten after that in four weeks.

TAKEAWAY: Creating SMART goals gives your plan critical details that will optimize your chances of success.

Lesson 30

Your Assets and Access

*Pulling a good network together takes
effort, sincerity, and time.*

~ Alan Collins

*The mark of a good conversationalist is
not that you can talk a lot. The mark is that you can
get others to talk a lot.*

~ Guy Kawasaki

When we decide what we want and put the previous mechanisms into place, we will develop a clear picture about how our assets and access can work for us.

When we talk about assets, society generally uses this term to reference financial or property holdings of some kind.

But here, in addition to finances, we're talking about all of the assets that make up our lives: our personality, characteristics, attributes, talents, knowledge, skills, abilities, strengths, opportunities, and so on.

In order to tap into these riches, we have to know what they are. *And, trust me, we have more assets than we give ourselves credit for.*

Access – or relationships with other people – is the totality of the networks we can tap into. When we have people in our lives that have wisdom and experience in the areas of our interest, we save ourselves massive amounts of time and heartache from having to reinvent the wheel. And it's a reminder that we don't have to go it alone.

Family; friends; neighbors; coworkers; church congregations; local business people; former classmates; and members of social, charity, and sports organizations make up just some of our access.

And our networks have networks of their own. *Trust me, we have more access than we give ourselves credit for.*

There's an added benefit to assets and access – the most important in my mind.

When we develop our assets as fully as possible, we learn more about ourselves and what we're capable of from the inside out. That is, it is our own voice, perspective, and beliefs that can contribute to the larger conversation, both now and in the future. We are in a position to give as much as we are willing to give.

When we develop our access as fully as possible, we're developing ongoing, meaningful relationships that enrich our lives. We learn more about ourselves and what we're capable of from the outside in. That is, it is others in our lives who show us the way. We're in a position to receive as much as we're willing to receive.

It's wonderful to have assets and access, but collecting them for the sake of collecting them is not what they're for. They exist to help us all get what we need. It's a symbiotic relationship.

Ultimately, understanding, developing, and using our assets and access helps to reduce fear. It shows the vast resources and support available to us. It provides experience, wisdom, and guidance. It demonstrates to ourselves what we're capable of.

Make a list of your assets and access, and see who you have in your life that can help you make the most of what you have inside you.

TAKEAWAY: Understanding the resources we already possess helps us see how to overcome the obstacles we fear are in our path.

Part 3

Action Mechanisms

Re-telling Your Story

This above all, to refuse to be a victim.

~ Margaret Atwood

To dare is to lose one's footing momentarily. Not to dare, is to lose oneself.

~ Soren Kierkegaard

We have spent some time creating mechanisms to help us assess our current situation. Now we have guidance that helps us jump off into the next stage: taking action.

People love stories. Just look at the success of Hollywood. A great story is built on well-developed characters, a gripping or poignant story we can relate to, and the profound transformation of the hero.

We're all storytellers with our own story to tell. The beauty of it is: we can choose which version we tell ourselves.

The story I chose to tell myself most often was one of anger, self-pity, and victimization, focusing on the things I didn't get in life. As a child, I wanted more attention and more affection and more togetherness delivered in a way that was meaningful to me.

Naturally, I didn't know anything about mortgages, bills, or the stress of raising twelve children. I was not equipped to consider that my parents may have had their own desires, dreams, and goals that may have gone unfulfilled. I had no idea what they may have sacrificed for my sake.

Like most of us, I interpreted what was happening around me at a time when I was not particularly good at interpreting. And I created the narrative of my life based on those interpretations. It was a narrative wrought with the fear that I wasn't deserving of love.

Over the years, I came to understand a couple of basic things:

- First, everyone has their own narrative and perspective on how life should be, and that's fine.
- Second, we're all delicate and sensitive with our own needs and fears.
- Third, I don't have to, and indeed can't, own others' interpretations or try to live by them.
- Fourth, and the biggest realization of all, I'm the one who made up my original narrative and can change it anytime I want.

I reworked – and continue to rework – my narrative to focus on the positive messages of the past to re-create myself. I re-interpreted my childhood, my parents, and most everything else around me to put fear into a different perspective, one that enabled me to create mechanisms to work through fear rather than being paralyzed by it or trying to destroy it.

It's easy to be blind to what we do have because we're so focused on what we don't have. Where in your story have you forgotten to see the good? What *did* you have in spite of what you didn't?

It's also difficult to see people for everything they are. No one is all good or all bad, even though we try to categorize them one way or the other. If all we can see is the bad in someone, we need to recognize that someone loves that person. What good things about them aren't we allowing ourselves to see through our lenses of fear?

Now it's your turn. Put pen to paper and re-invent yourself. Revisit the Lessons in Part II and rewrite your narrative based not on your past suffering but on your future self, on the dreams you want to live.

TAKEAWAY: It's your story. You get to choose if it's filled with love and happiness.

Disprove the Negative Messages

*No one can make you feel inferior without
your consent.*

~ Eleanor Roosevelt

*Technology is not going to save us.
Our computers, our tools, our machines are
not enough. We have to rely on our
intuition, our true being.*

~ Joseph Campbell

One of the mechanisms we can create in our lives that speaks directly to addressing fear and re-telling our story is learning to disprove the negative messages of the past.

Through our narrative construction in childhood, we came to believe our interpretations of the environment in which we found ourselves. We believed that these interpretations were us. But they weren't; they were simply one possible way of looking at the situation. Our interpretations were our versions of what happened.

In the course of re-writing our narratives, we want to actively engage in disproving the negative messages, looking for new interpretations.

For example, in his wonderful book, *Freedom from Fear*, Howard Liebgold presents the following negative core belief:

> "My father said, 'Any man that works with his hands is a failure.' I work with my hands – therefore, I am a failure."

We know the messages we receive from authority figures, especially parents, can be potent, burned into our memories, and an influence on the meaning we give ourselves. The insidious nature of fear is we often become blind to solutions and options when we're in the grips of its destructive power. Essentially, we're prisoners behind bars of our own making that we can remove when we decide to remove them.

Liebgold presents ways to disprove the negative core belief mentioned above:

"My dad was wrong. His definition of failure was far too limited."

"He was probably just trying to steer me to another profession."

"By his definition, all farmers, carpenters, plumbers, machinists, mechanics, and repairmen are failures. That's ridiculous."

"You don't define human beings by their vocation alone."

"I am a successful foreman, an accomplished inventor, a staunch supporter of my church, a great father and grandfather."

"I am not on this earth to measure up to anyone's expectations, including my father's."

"If I disappointed him, too bad. He'll have to deal with it."

"My dad has never called me a failure. I wonder if I took his statement out of context."

When we engage in this process of reframing, we choose to change our vision and release our poisonous emotions, like anger, self-pity, and victimization that may have been attached to it. We approach this exercise with empathy and forgiveness toward our current selves, our childhood selves, and the people we identified as the deliverers of the messages.

Our job is to assume that every negative belief we held is wrong. We're now looking at our lives – and our fears – with a fresh set of eyes. We are bringing a different perspective to our childhood interpretations – that of an adult.

TAKEAWAY: Take the power out of negative beliefs by disproving them.

Lesson 33

Your Hot Air Balloon

*One day your life will flash before your eyes. Make
sure it's worth watching.*

~ Unknown

*Death is not the greatest loss in life. The greatest
loss is what dies inside us while we live.*

~ Norman Cousins

When we're fearful, we sometimes surround ourselves by things and people that aren't helping us get closer to our goal. We have cluttered spaces and negative influences.

Once we've started the lifelong exercise of reflecting on the questions who am I, want do I want, and how am I going to get it, we can take stock of where we are today.

We don't need to beat ourselves up over bad decisions or focus on ways we were treated unjustly. As Chinese farmers, we are now thinking: It is what it is; now, what good can we bring from it?

We remind ourselves that the R in SMART goals stands for Results-oriented. Now that we have started to rewrite our narrative and learned how to disprove the negative messages around us, we have to move toward organizing our physical world. This is primarily a de-clutter phase. (We'll talk in greater detail about this in another book in the *Get the Nerve™ Series, Time Management*.)

A simple de-clutter exercise helps us gain momentum, gives us a quick sense of accomplishment, and drive fear downward.

One exercise I use to illustrate this in my programs is the hot air balloon.

The instructions are simple: We are each in our own hot air balloon that is weighed down by a considerable amount of junk we have accumulated over the years as well as negative people who are draining our energy, time, and passion. If we don't take action, our balloon will crash in ten minutes. If it crashes, we will not survive. Our task is to write a list and then take action. What are the things we need to throw overboard?

Now we look at that list and decide what we can do right now. Make the bed? Empty the garbage pails? Clean out a junk drawer? Pick up clothes from the floor? Throw out a couple of things from the garage? Just choose one thing and do it.

Fear creeps in and stays when we have the habit of trying to accomplish everything at once. Even the smartest, most talented individuals can't do that. Successful people do what's possible at this moment; they don't try to do everything.

On our list we also have named some people who reinforce our outdated narratives from childhood. They may be locked down in their own struggle with fear and treat us in a negative way, or they simply may have no idea they have that impact on us. The bottom line, though, is you trained them how to treat you by accepting certain behaviors.

If you don't like the way people relate to you, let them know in a polite yet firm way that you're tired of it. If it's a superficial habit, they may acknowledge it and change it. If it's a deep-seated part of their personality, you will have to make a decision about continuing to interact with that person. Two things to keep in mind: First, you can't change anyone else. Second, *you* may be the reason people treat you the way they do.

TAKEAWAY: Take time to de-clutter your space, time, and relationships in order to reduce fear.

Lesson 34
Create Your SMART Goal

You are never too old to set another goal or to dream a new dream.

~ C. S. Lewis

The difference between who you are and who you want to be is what you do.

~ Bill Phillips

Hopefully, we've been thinking throughout this book about what we would do if we had no fear. We've thought about our pasts and started to re-write our narratives. We figured out how to disprove the negative messages we've bombarded ourselves with throughout our lives. And we've started clearing out some of the clutter and toxic people around us.

That's a great start to getting fear under control.

In Part II on Assessment Mechanisms, we talked about the nature of goals and the characteristics of a SMART goal. Now, in this section on taking action, we're going to create a goal.

Write down one goal you are going to achieve.

As always, we assess the quality of the stated goal with a series of questions.

Is it Specific? Measurable? Attainable? Results-oriented? Time-bound? If not, how can you make it more so?

Now that it's a SMART goal, what next steps do you need to take to move toward achieving it?

What tools or resources do you need in order to achieve your goal? Does it require money? Equipment? Work space? Assistance from other people?

Now, assign a specific deadline when each step needs to be completed.

When is the optimal time to work on these steps?

How will you minimize interruptions when you're working on your goal? When they happen, how will you handle them?

What does "done" look like? How will you know when you've completed your goal? You may think it's self-evident, but it's a good practice to state it explicitly so there are no surprises at the end.

I know this is not fun. I resisted doing these exercises for years. Guess what? There's no way around them. If this is what successful people do, if doing exercises is the requirement of working in spite of ourselves, we have to do them.

As a recovering perfectionist and a long-suffering procrastinator, I have come to the conclusion that the vast majority of tasks I avoided for weeks, months, and years, were not nearly as complicated as my mind made them out to be. This may be because I never put in place SMART goals; I just let life happen to me.

I made a lot of missteps and missed a lot of opportunities. It didn't have to be this way for me and it doesn't have to be that way for you.

Take some time to answer the questions in writing. With details in place, the scariest part of reaching your goal will be done.

TAKEAWAY: Set SMART goals to overcome fear and make progress recreating your life.

Lesson 35

Filter Out the Fear

*Dwelling on the negative simply contributes to
its power.*

~ Shirley MacLaine

*Have respect for yourself, and patience and
compassion. With these, you can handle anything.*

~ Jack Kornfield

One of the most potent mechanisms we can develop in our toolkit is the filter. A filter is one of the mechanisms that can very effectively keep fear in perspective. If we remember E + R = O, applying the filter happens in that space between the Event and our Response. It is the space where growth occurs, as Viktor Frankl said (Lesson 11).

Filters remind us of what we own and what other people own. It's important not to confuse the two.

When we use filters, so many situations we may have used to create drama in our lives are suddenly transformed. Moments that were laced with fear in the past now become just moments.

We are Chinese farmers who live by the mantra, "It is what it is; now, what good can we bring from it?"

One of the many times I've used filters was at the conference I mentioned in Lesson 19. I was working as an organizer and host of conferences and seminars. It was my fifth day at the job. In other words, I had no idea what I was doing.

Remember how the woman told me in front of everyone that I was no good at my job?

At least that is the way I would have interpreted it had I not had my filter in place. I would have been embarrassed and used the situation as yet more proof that "I am not good enough." However, I had learned over the years that no one can embarrass me; I can only choose to be embarrassed by hanging on to my fears.

As soon as the conference attendee stood up, my filters automatically activated:

- She chose to stand up and say something. That wasn't about me.
- She chose the words to say. That wasn't about me.
- She chose the tone she used. That wasn't about me.
- She had given me nothing to respond to and no reason to be embarrassed. So far, none of what she said or did was about me. I was simply waiting to find out what actually had to be fixed.

Finally, she made her point about the conference, and then I had a choice to make. I could either get angry at her for calling me out in front of everyone or I could thank her for pointing out the inadequacies of the conference.

The filters help me to understand what is mine to own and what is not mine to own. They keep the Chinese farmer front of mind: "It is what it is; now, what good can we bring from it?"

TAKEAWAY: Apply filters to better understand what's happening around you so you can choose the most appropriate responses.

Lesson 36
Manage Your Chatterbox

If you judge people, you have no time to love them.

~ Mother Teresa

*The way you treat yourself sets the standard
for others.*

~ Sonya Friedman

Our internal chatterbox will reflect our perspective on ourselves and the world, and, in turn, it will reveal our fears. Are we perfectionists or optimalists? If we fall short of a goal, do the chatterbox voices in our mind call us a failure?

We can reframe our thoughts.

Sometimes it takes having optimistic, passionate, and supportive people around us to reframe our thoughts. Sometimes evidence that our voices and our interpretations are wrong can help reframe our thoughts.

We can change our thoughts in an instant and then work toward changing our mechanisms and our actions.

My chatterbox told me countless negative things like "I'm terrible at...," "Nobody wants me...," "I'm not smart enough...," "I'm not good enough...," "I don't measure up...."

One particularly potent dismissive message was, "Well, if I know something then everyone knows it. I don't need to share it with anybody." This script was a total discounting of what I was capable of and what I could share with the world.

One of the many problems with the chatterbox is that when we make ourselves a slave to it, it has a way of keeping us frozen in place. We can't be of service to other people. We can't live our potential and fulfill the promise the universe bestowed on us.

Is your chatterbox telling you that you have to be the hero, that you have to get people's attention, in order to be validated? Do you think this is actually true?

Is your chatterbox telling you to brag about your exploits so people can see you and validate you? Do you think people really enjoy hearing about this for the umpteenth time?

Is your chatterbox telling you that you have to put people down in order to feel better about yourself? Do you think this makes you look like anything but a mean person?

I used to think the chatterbox was a bad thing and needed to be silenced once and for all. But I've reached the point of listening to it rather than pushing it away. I want to make the voices orderly, sort them out, understand what they are saying, figure out where they're coming from, and question the assumptions, beliefs, and claims behind them.

In this way, I can try to minimize or even remove the emotion from the voices, re-write my narrative, and create a plan for moving forward.

TAKEAWAY: Rein in the voices in your mind so you can learn from them and change them.

Learn to Love the Plateau

If people knew how hard I worked to get my mastery, it wouldn't seem so wonderful at all.

~ Michelangelo

In the realm of ideas everything depends on enthusiasm; in the real world all rests on perseverance.

~ Johann Wolfgang von Goethe

When we try something new, our first steps are frequently filled with mixed emotions. We're excited about the prospect of a new beginning. Doors are opening that hadn't before.

We're stretching and growing and dreaming about possibility. We set out on a steep learning curve and seem to be absorbing so much very quickly. It's exciting and fun.

At the same time, we can feel anxious, uncertain, clumsy, and filled with trepidation. After all, learning something new can be scary. It will force us to leave our comfort zone.

We're taking a chance putting ourselves out there because most of us have been conditioned to worry about failure. "What if I make a mistake?" "What if I just can't do it?"

All of that is OK because nothing great ever happens without leaving our comfort zone and making mistakes.

After a while, though – whether we're learning a new skill or trying to lose weight – it will seem we're not making as much progress as we had been. The excitement and novelty of our new venture starts to wear off, and we become frustrated when we hit a plateau.

While it may feel like we have stalled, this is actually a natural occurrence. We can't remain on a steady, upward path; there will be ebbs and flows in our progress.

The challenge is to recognize when we hit a plateau and understand what it really means.

The plateau – especially the first one – is where many of us give in to our frustration and simply quit.

With a mindset of frustration, impatience, and fear, it can be difficult to realize that another leap of progress is waiting up ahead.

The trick is to understand that plateaus happen, and fairly often. We have to be prepared that the chatterbox will raise its voice and say, "See, I told you this was going to be impossible."

When successful people reach the plateau, they simply keeping going – without judgment, second-guessing, or quitting – and continue to work.

They understand that plateaus are a natural part of any progress.

They also know that plateaus are an important part of the process of continuous learning.

Plateaus allow our brains time to digest and make sense of what we're working on, preparing us for the next leap of progress.

When we hit a plateau, we should be excited! Just around the corner is our next leap forward.

TAKEAWAY: Understanding and welcoming plateaus is a critical part of overcoming your fear of stepping outside your comfort zone.

Break It Down

*You can only grow if you're willing to feel awkward
and uncomfortable when you try something new.*

~ Brian Tracy

*It is better to make many small steps in
the right direction than to make a great leap
forward only to stumble backward.*

~ Proverb

Our fear can easily get activated when we look at the totality – the enormity – of the task before us. One of the best mechanisms for dealing with fear in the face of an overwhelming, complex project is to break it down.

When we break down our goal, our complex task, into as many smaller pieces as possible, it makes the pieces more digestible. That is, it begins to reduce the sense of being overwhelmed; it begins to reduce the fear of not being able to do it all. We are now tackling just one small piece at a time.

To paraphrase Creighton Abrams, How do you eat an elephant? One bite at a time.

We have many different ways of dealing with this, depending on how our brains are wired and depending on what kind of learner we are. Some of us draw diagrams, pictures, or charts. Some visualize. Some read what others write about complex tasks, and how to tackle them.

In my Time Management program, I use a guitar to show the audience how they can learn to play in five minutes. There's no trick or gimmick.

The key to the exercise is to change the audience's perspective. Instead of looking at the whole guitar, we isolate our focus to just a few notes arranged in a very simple pattern. We break it down.

Bringing that kind of perspective to everything we do, we can accomplish more than we might have thought otherwise possible.

The same thing applied when I was writing this book.

If I focused only on the fact that I had to "write a book," it would've been very overwhelming.

So I had to change my perspective. "I'm not writing a book," I said to myself, "I'm writing a lot of small essays. And I can only write one essay at a time."

If I wanted a very low-stress experience writing it, I could have easily written one essay per day. Each lesson is about 400 words. If I were committed to doing that every single day, it would have taken me fifty days to do the first draft.

In my previous life, I would have spent longer than that just worrying about the project.

When we break down the task in front of us, the task becomes much easier, and we decrease the probability of activating our fear and dragging our feet on the project or never starting it at all.

TAKEAWAY: Break down every goal or project into manageable pieces.

Get the Right Tools for the Job

*Man is a tool-using animal. Without tools he is
nothing, with tools he is all.*

~ Thomas Carlyle

*We become what we behold. We shape our tools and
then our tools shape us.*

~ Marshall McLuhan

One of the big lessons I learned over the years was the importance of having the right tools for the job.

Sometimes we want to take shortcuts and try to speed up a process that really shouldn't be sped up. Or we don't want to take the time required to really set up our operation before launching it. Fear and overwhelm frequently result when we do that.

The right tools applied to the right mechanism makes work easier, reduces time wasted, and decreases the opportunities for fear to seep inside us. When we have a plan and the right tools, we can set off to work.

It took me a long time to get the nerve to get a Ph.D. The only reason I didn't do it when I could have was fear, plain and simple. I *believed* I couldn't do it, and therefore I couldn't.

One of the jobs I had at the university during the Ph.D. program was as editor-in-chief of an international crime magazine that was distributed to twenty-five countries. Actually, I had volunteered to take on the task. The only problem was I'd never worked at a magazine, let alone run one. I was scared.

The usual fears arose: what if I fail? What if people criticize me? What if I make mistakes? Of course, people criticized me and I made plenty of mistakes.

I started working on the magazine in a very haphazard way. There were stacks of paper all over my desk. With school work on my mind and other projects on my plate, it was impossible to keep track of the material for the magazine. Stress increased, and more fear came rolling in.

I realized that I didn't have the right tools for the job. I didn't have the right tools to stop the onslaught of paper and emails coming at me. I wasn't organized.

The first thing I did was get a system of stacked mailboxes and a label maker. I put all the material for each article in its own box. In no time I had a simple tool to help the magazine mechanism work well, smoothly, and the fear diminished greatly. It also happened to be a great time saver, and the quality of the magazine improved.

Sometimes the issue of fear and addressing our fears is exacerbated by a lack of organization. Sometimes we don't understand what the right tools are because we haven't defined our goal clearly and specifically enough.

The right tools for the job make it easier to get started.

Take stock of your environment, checking to see if you have all of the right tools for the task you're trying to accomplish. You may need to spend a little money. Don't think twice about it. It will save you time and aggravation, dramatically reducing your fear.

TAKEAWAY: The right tools make the job easier and lower your frustration so you're more likely to succeed.

Work with an Accountability Coach

Collaboration is THE critical competency for achieving and sustaining high performance.

~ Jim Kouzes and Barry Posner

Every excuse I ever heard made perfect sense to the person who made it.

~ Daniel Drubin

We all know that setting our own SMART goals and sticking to them sometimes requires a feat of strength we don't always possess. We vow to watch TV for thirty minutes and we sit for three hours. We swear off chocolate cake only to indulge at the next birthday party. You know the drill.

We don't want to feel embarrassed. We don't want to look stupid. We don't want to go through the painful experience of stepping outside our comfort zone. Our answer is to go it alone to avoid the discomfort. But going it alone means slow and uneven progress, if any. One step forward and two – or three – steps back.

We need a mechanism of accountability. We need an outside force who will help us turn around our fears, questions, negativity, and doubts. We need a motivator.

We can call the motivator in our lives a coach, mentor, counselor, partner, friend – anything we want – as long as the process is active, engaged, and effective.

The motivator is there to make sure the goals we set are SMART, to help us determine realistic deadlines that will also make us stretch, and to see us victorious in being bold and living the dream.

"Accountability" can be such an ugly word. We might think being held accountable is a fear-inducing process. Just that phrase – "being held accountable" – is scary because it's been used over time in fairly frightening, negative ways in connection with punishment. Forget about that. Accountability is our new best friend.

The fact of the matter is, as human beings, we have plenty of weaknesses. We often give in to the various temptations around us and we need a mechanism to change that.

Accountability is nothing more than a way to encourage us to be better today than we were yesterday. Our coach is someone who shows us effective techniques, helps us through difficult periods, and celebrates with us. When we compete with our yesterday self with a coach by our side, we dig deeper than we would otherwise.

Right now, even though I provide accountability workshops, I have two accountability coaches I speak with every two weeks. They propel not only my progress, but also my entire team's, in writing books, getting speaking engagements, conducting workshops, managing social media, and all of the other activities we pursue.

In case there are any lingering doubts, let's be clear about something: Having an accountability coach is not a weakness; it's about ensuring we get the results we want. It's a powerful mechanism to put fear in its place while we live the dream.

TAKEAWAY: Collaboration and accountability will help you reach your goals faster.

Part 4

A Seven-Step Success Plan for Overcoming Fear

Step 1 – Acknowledge Your Fear

*Acknowledging fear is not a cause for depression
or discouragement.... The essence of cowardice is not
acknowledging the reality of fear.*

~ Chogyam Trungpa

*A rock pile ceases to be a rock pile the
moment a single man contemplates it, bearing
within him
the image of a cathedral.*

~ Antoine de Saint-Exupery

As we draw near to the end of this book, we can create for ourselves a straightforward, seven-step success plan for overcoming fear that frames and utilizes everything we discussed in the preceding pages.

Frequently, we avoid facing fear because fear itself is scary.

Acknowledging fear may mean admitting we're less in control than we or others think. We may believe people will look at us differently, perhaps less charitably, knowing we're afraid.

The first step in doing anything about fear is to acknowledge its presence.

We've been doing a lot of thinking over the past forty lessons. Let's stop for just a moment and take a deep breath, followed by a long, slow exhale. This is a time to pause and sit peacefully, quieting our minds, pushing the daily grind of the rat race out of our heads.

Gently, and in a spirit of self-forgiveness and self-acknowledgement, we say to ourselves, "Yes, I am afraid."

"Yes, I am afraid. I embrace my human imperfection. I recognize myself and call myself by that which I am: vulnerable, sensitive, deserving, worthy."

"Yes, I am afraid. My fears don't define me. My fears don't make me less. My fears don't equate to lack in my life. It is what it is. Now, what good can we bring from it?"

"Yes, I am afraid. I now have to live my life on my own terms. I no longer have the protection of blaming others or making excuses. It is scary, but it is the best way forward, the only way forward."

We're human, and it is the nature of the beast to be afraid. There is nothing wrong with experiencing fear. We have our fears, just like everyone else has their fears. We don't need to judge our insides by others' outsides. We can relax into the thought that everyone is afraid.

We need not worry if others criticize us for acknowledging our own fears; their opinion is none of our business. We need not worry if others fail to acknowledge their own fears; let them be.

Acknowledging fear is the first step on the road to doing something about it. The result may be to realize that we are confused about who we are, what we want, and how we're going to get it.

That's OK. We're human. Confusion is the prelude to clarity. It's the first step in facing the brutal facts and creating a mindset for change. It's not an indication of weakness. It's a sign that we may have to change something in our lives. It is what it is.

TAKEAWAY: We shouldn't forsake fulfilling the potential of our lives for fear of acknowledging our fear.

Step 2 – Identify Your Fear

*The real voyage of discovery consists not in seeking
new landscapes, but in having new eyes.*

~ Marcel Proust

*We are all humiliated by the sudden discovery of
a fact which has existed very comfortably and
perhaps been staring at us in private while we have
been making up our world entirely without it.*

~ George Eliot

What is it *exactly* we're afraid of?

I mean that quite literally. Let's stop and ask ourselves exactly what it is we're afraid of.

Over the past few years, I have been asking audiences in my programs what they're afraid of. After they tell me the inevitable spiders, snakes, heights, and the dentist, I ask them to go a little deeper. On a more fundamental level, what are people afraid of?

As we discussed in Lesson 1, the list is a fairly predictable, perhaps even universal one. The top ten fears people have, according to my audiences, are: 1. Making mistakes. 2. Being embarrassed. 3. Failure. 4. Success. 5. Rejection. 6. Criticism. 7. The unknown. 8. Losing freedom. 9. Disappointment. 10. Being forgotten.

I also ask what people want. The initial responses typically deal with material items: big houses, a lot of money, a nice car. After that, I ask them to go a little deeper. On a more fundamental level, what do people want?

Eventually we get to a list of three things: 1. People want to be heard. 2. People want to be respected. 3. People want to be loved. Other desires could be identified, but I think that's a pretty good list.

Do your fears come from one of those three things being absent? Are you afraid of not being loved? Are you afraid you won't be heard? Are you afraid you won't be respected?

In order to identify our fears, we really need to take a hard look at ourselves. Remember, it always starts with us and our self-awareness. We can try to avoid identifying our fears, but they have a way of showing up, if not directly then indirectly.

How are our fears showing up in our lives? Are we even aware that many of our actions and reactions to the world around us may be based on our own fears?

Is our communication style reflecting our fears? Do we yell or criticize to cover up our fears of not being enough?

Do our eating habits reflect our fears? Do we eat when we're bored or upset to cover up fears of being alone, imperfect, or without purpose?

Do we micro-manage the people around us as part of our personal fear of losing control and being seen as a failure?

It's time we strip down some of the protective shell and bring some of our fears into the light. Whether through reflection and contemplation, conversation, or assistance from professional counselors, identifying fears and how they manifest in our daily lives is a game changer.

TAKEAWAY: We must know what we're facing before we can overcome it.

Step 3 – Measure Your Fear

Tell your heart that the fear of suffering is worse
than the suffering itself. And that no heart has
ever suffered when it goes in search of its dreams,
because every second of the search is a second's
encounter with God and with eternity.

~ Paulo Coelho

Tired of lying in the sunshine
Staying home to watch the rain
You are young and life is long
And there is time to kill today
And then one day you find
Ten years have got behind you
No one told you when to run
You missed the starting gun

~ Pink Floyd

How many times have we been afraid of a task we needed to complete or a conversation we needed to have and put it off for days, weeks, or even months? How about years?

When we finally summon the courage to face what scares us, we often find it takes a fraction of the time to complete than we anticipated, and hardly any of our worst fears actually occur.

We need to short circuit that process; it's time consuming and serves to prolong and deepen our fear. When the next scary project comes up, we'll resort to our old ways unless we get the nerve to do something different.

The mechanism for changing that approach to our fear is fairly straightforward: Measure the fear.

When we're afraid of something, we can put it on a scale of one to ten, with ten being the thing we fear most in life.

Most of our fears will likely come in below six or seven. When we look at it that way, we show ourselves that we can handle it.

When we measure something, we're trying to find out how much there is of a specific thing. We give it context, proportion, and scale in order to understand it better.

Measuring is a necessity because fear has tricky properties. The longer fear stays in our minds, the worse it gets. It often mutates into something unrecognizable from our original fear. Our chatterbox urges it to grow even more until it overpowers us, strangles our confidence, and paralyzes us.

We intensify the situation by not sharing our fear with anybody. We're afraid of what they will say to us or think about us, and we end up depriving ourselves of a release valve. Before we know it, years have passed and we haven't lived the dream.

I find one of the most effective ways to measure my fear is to notice what others are accomplishing in spite of having less than me. "I'm worried about embarrassing myself? Look at that man over there. He has no arms and yet he's living all his dreams."

My fear can be transformed from a nine or ten to a two or three simply by regaining focus for one second. I'm not measuring my worth against someone else; I'm creating the courage to tackle my fear by putting it in perspective.

TAKEAWAY: When fear appears, we quickly measure it in order to find the courage to keep moving forward.

Lesson 44

Step 4 – Determine the Worst Case

We either learn to fail or we fail to learn.

~ Tal Ben-Shahar

When trying to make a decision, I often think of the worst case scenario. I call it 'the eaten by wolves factor.' If I do something, what's the most terrible thing that could happen? Would I be eaten by wolves? One thing that makes it possible to be an optimist is if you have a contingency plan for when all hell breaks loose. There are a lot of things I don't worry about, because I have a plan in place if they do.

~ Randy Pausch

Once we have measured our fear, giving it proportion and context, we can ask the next essential question: What's the worst thing that could happen?

This is a serious question, integral to our SWOT analysis, and needs to be explored. What are the consequences I would suffer if my worst fears were to come true?

It should be noted that the very fact we've spent time creating Assessment Mechanisms (Part II) and Action Mechanisms (Part III) means we're now in a much better position to deal with fear.

We now have concrete steps to take when fear starts to become an obstacle to our progress. We know how to rewrite our narrative and disprove negative messages. We can filter our fear and break down complex tasks to reduce fear.

We will not be looking at fear with the same mind we had before reading this book.

We know where fear comes from, how it manifests itself, and the myths surrounding it. We know it is more emotion than fact. We know we can manage it.

As a result, we have transformed the way we think about worst case scenarios. Our knowledge of fear is empowering. Instead of fear being paralyzing, it now becomes helpful to us in our planning. We are now equipped to analyze the possible scenarios more clearly, with less influence from the biases of fear.

This is not to say fear has disappeared, but we're in a better position to suppress our ego and plan more rationally than we might have otherwise.

When I started my company as a speaker, trainer, and writer, I went through this exercise myself with a series of questions. If a program doesn't go well, what is the worst thing that could happen? How do I anticipate the worst, plan for it, and not allow the possibility of failure to deter me?

If my books get terrible reviews or don't sell well, what is the worst thing that could happen, and how can I adapt to that reality?

What if I am forced to close down my business? What is the worst thing that could happen?

When we answer these kinds of questions, we now have more information, contingency plans, alternatives, and ways to reduce fear.

None of these events – failed programs, terrible reviews, closing the business down – would be an evaluation of me as a person. I don't have to worry about people's reactions should these worst case scenarios occur. Nor will these events result in outrageous losses – I won't lose my wife, my friends, my home, or my ability to find a new job.

As with all of us, the testament to who I am as a person will be in the way I respond to these challenges.

TAKEAWAY: The fear of worst case scenarios becomes less potent when we have a plan in place and don't believe in unrealistic extremes.

Step 5 – Collect Information and Elicit Support

*A fine glass vase goes from treasure to trash, the
moment it is broken. Fortunately, something else
happens to you and me. Pick up your pieces. Then,
help me gather mine.*

~ Vera Nazarian

*Encourage life, and strengthen one another.
For the positive energy spread to one will be felt by
us all. For we are connected, one and all.*

~ Deborah Day

Information and support have been at the core of building and acting on the mechanisms we put in place.

When we create our Wheel of Life, analyze our SWOT, and set a SMART goal, we are collecting information about ourselves, exploring our fears, and coming to terms with what we want. We're questioning our beliefs, assumptions, experiences, and our narratives to increase our awareness.

Keep in mind that we can collect information related to our fear from a multitude of sources: books, online resources, people, lyrics and poetry, museums, reflections on our past experiences, our heart, and using this seven-step success plan, among others.

I frequently use books on fear, psychology, spirituality, and other related topics to shift my perspective on fear.

For many years I believed I could never lose weight. One day I tried something different. I read just one diet and exercise book, set up a SMART goal, and Decided and Committed to do everything the author suggested. I lost fifteen lbs. in six weeks with no problem. I lost another ten after that. The fears surrounding weight loss subsequently disappeared.

This shouldn't surprise anyone. We already know how to succeed; we often just lack the discipline to do what needs to be done. This is simply another example of fear – fear of hard work, fear of failure, fear of success, or something else along these lines.

In addition to collecting information, a great way to face our fear is by having support. It's extremely difficult to try to analyze our fears alone and expect to have the best perspective. The viewpoint of a supportive person is invaluable.

We need someone who understands what we're trying to accomplish. We don't need pessimists, critics, naysayers, or anyone else who will hold us back. We need support. It could be a family member, friend, clergy, athletic coach, life coach, executive coach, or therapist, virtually any person who can educate us and motivate us. This person can also be your accountability coach.

If we quickly dismiss the idea of having a support coach, watch a professional football game. Coaches clutter the sidelines. If someone who is highly trained and makes millions of dollars needs coaches, we do too. Coaches provide support, information, guidance, discipline, encouragement, and even direction.

That's why we attend classes at gyms and hire personal trainers. That's why corporate executives enlist business coaches. It's why we go to therapy, church, school, get tutors, and so on. They're all coaches, and they show us how to play the game – whether its football, business, or life.

I agreed to do a twenty-one-day sugar detox with my wife. The first week was very difficult, and I never would have succeeded without her. The fact that we did it together made all the difference. Setting ourselves up for success with the help of another person is a powerful mechanism to bring to our battle with fear.

TAKEAWAY: When we seek out information from experts and the support of knowledgeable, positive people, we set ourselves up for success.

Step 6 – Reflect on Past Success

Success is how high you bounce when you hit bottom.

~ George S. Patton

Success is to be measured not so much by the position that one has reached in life as by the obstacles which he has overcome.

~ Booker T. Washington

All of us have had success of one kind or other at some point in our lives. It doesn't matter whether it was big or small, we've had it.

It started from infancy. We successfully crawled across the floor. Then we tried to stand up. We fell down. We stood up again. We fell down. Finally, we stood up and didn't fall down. Success! Before long we were walking, first on shaky legs and then more confidently.

We acquired language. We made friends. We learned basic skills. We take these for granted. They just happened, we say. We had no choice, we say. We didn't have any say in the matter. We just did them. Yes! That's the point! We have a track record of just doing things – we watched people around us, we got help from parents and teachers, and we just did them. We were successful. In fact, we were successful a *lot* of times.

At this stage in our lives we're doing the same thing. We may have to be more selective about who we watch for inspiration, who helps us, and who we keep around, but it's the same process: take instruction from successful coaches we trust, do what they say, fall down, get up, fall down, learn to walk. Decide. Commit. Succeed.

We already have everything we need. We just need to be reminded that success is possible. We just need to be reminded that it's about the process. And we just need to be reminded that fear didn't stop us in the past; we did what we needed to do.

Think about the thousands of successes you've had in life.

In my transition period, when I was moving from being paralyzed to being courageous, I set up a praise file. This was a collection of emails, cards, notes, photos, report cards, excellent school papers, anything thanking me for a job well done, congratulating me on an achievement, acknowledging my effort, or simply telling me I made someone's day.

I kept the praise file close by and used it actively. I added to it as often as possible.

This was the perfect mechanism to undermine my fear, at least long enough to get through the project or task that was scaring me. When I felt myself stalling, I pulled open the desk drawer, plucked out the file, and read a couple of the notes.

Before long I could say to myself, "I've done this before. I know how this works. Let's get on with it" or "I've succeeded a lot in the past at things that were more difficult than this. I got this." It was a great counterbalance to the Bully in my head that kept reminding me I wasn't good enough or that it was too dangerous to take risks.

Think about the most difficult thing you have done or accomplished in life you didn't think would be possible. Take a few minutes to remember it and give yourself credit.

TAKEAWAY: Constantly remind yourself how successful you've been so you know how capable you are.

Step 7 – Celebrate

The more you praise and celebrate your life,
the more there is in life to celebrate.

~ Oprah Winfrey

I have arrived, I am home/In the here, in the now/
I am solid, I am free/In the ultimate I dwell.

~ Thich Nhat Hanh

My audiences find celebration to be a most unexpected topic in my presentations, and yet they nod their heads in obvious agreement. They know how important it is to celebrate, and they also know we all do it far too infrequently.

Perhaps there's something embarrassing about celebrating our own wins. People may look at us and think our egos have gotten out of control. They may judge that what we accomplished is not worthy of celebration. As I mentioned earlier, their opinion of us is none of our business.

The real problem is we don't celebrate enough. Research shows that praising other people – celebrating their victories, their accomplishments, their efforts – is one of the most important factors in job satisfaction, staff retention, and other critical organizational issues.

And I'm willing to bet praise is no less critical at home. In fact, my wife is asking me to tell you that's true. She wants you to know how much she appreciates it that I celebrate all of her wins. She says it helps her acknowledge her own unique gifts and believe in herself more.

I'm also reminded of wise words a friend of mine once said: "Sometimes you have to give yourself what you didn't get from others." So don't be embarrassed: Celebrate. Praise yourself and others.

Celebrating small wins helps to acknowledge our victory and builds momentum toward the next task at hand, especially one we're afraid of. All too often we diminish the things we accomplish as nothing special or something everyone can do.

The Bully voice used to be strong in my mind, saying, "Well, if you could do it, anyone can do it." And I listened. No celebrating. No praise. What I do doesn't matter.

Here's the thing about celebrating: It's an important link in the chain that carries us more easily from task to task, victory to victory, as we put fear in perspective.

Overcoming fear is not about anybody but you. It's about you being better today than you were yesterday.

Celebrating is a chance for us to remind ourselves that we can achieve far more than we thought possible.

Get off your own back.

Your most recent success may be relatively small in everyone else's eyes, but it should be big for you. Only you know the effort and maybe even the anguish it took to face yourself, and your fears, in order to accomplish this thing.

We set ourselves up for success.

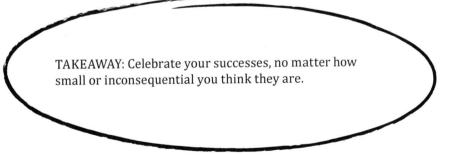

TAKEAWAY: Celebrate your successes, no matter how small or inconsequential you think they are.

Part 5

Living the Dream

100% Responsibility for Your Choices

*My life and my work have taught me that
freedom from fear has nothing to do with being
rid of fear, and everything to do with
making conscious, healthy choices about how we will
respond in the presence of fear.*

~ Thom Rutledge

*Everything you do is based on the choices you make.
It's not your parents, your past relationships,
your job, the economy, the weather, an argument
or your age that is to blame. You and only you are
responsible for every decision and choice you make.
Period.*

~ Brenda Slavin

So much of our fear comes from our failure to take 100% responsibility for our own choices.

We hang on to narratives from decades ago, angry over things we were given, things we weren't given, the way someone looked at us, or the fact that someone didn't look at us at all. We've built up so many defensive devices they've become our mode of operation. It's difficult to see they're keeping us from living the dream.

One of the best mechanisms to push us into a reflex of taking 100% responsibility for our choices is what I call "falling on your sword." It is best to quickly acknowledge wrong doing, mistakes, or misunderstandings and remove them as obstacles on your road. If we can develop the habit of doing it automatically when the situation calls for it, it will save time, anxiety, and hurt feelings.

When we dig our heels in to defend our position – especially when we're wrong – we can be pretty sure there's fear lurking behind those feelings. When we insist on being right all the time or constantly correcting people, there's a lot of fear involved. If we're going to fight tooth and nail to be recognized, that involves fear as well.

This fight is proof we are not taking 100% responsibility for our choices. It's the expression of self-protection and ego. "Falling on our sword" helps remove obstacles to open and honest communication.

It's impossible to make conscious, healthy choices if we don't find out what the options are and we don't know where we want to go. These choices, cloaked in responsibility, concern every single aspect of our lives – every category in the Wheel of Life.

We are where we are because we didn't plan, and execute a plan, to be anywhere else.

I was delivering a program once when one of the participants approached me during a break. She said she was fifty years old and was the first person in her family to go to college. She had been a criminal justice major and was now working as a probation officer. She discovered over the years her real passion was in another area, having nothing to do with criminal justice. She didn't want to pursue it because it would hurt her parents' feelings. She felt guilty because of the sacrifice her parents had made and was afraid to make the move. She was not taking 100% responsibility for her own choices. She's still in that job.

Think in advance and decide that no matter what comes, we will step up and take responsibility – for our pasts, our presents, and our futures. When we take 100% responsibility for our choices, it becomes easier to move forward.

TAKEAWAY: Develop the habit of falling on your sword and taking 100% responsibility for how your life is turning out.

Lesson 49

Forgiveness

Forgiveness is a virtue of the brave.

~ Indira Gandhi

To forgive is to set a prisoner free and discover that the prisoner was you.

~ Lewis B. Smedes

In my teen years, I never placed value on learning to drive. I didn't need to.

First, I was the ninth of twelve; there was always a sibling-chauffeur to be found.

Second, I was afraid of it, as I was afraid of most things. I didn't believe I could do it.

Consequently, I never quite fully knew how all the roads connected; some were hazy to me, as if on foreign territory.

As it would happen, after being away from home for some twenty years, I found myself back there. I took a job as a taxi driver for a few months on those very same streets.

One day I was shuttling between the town I grew up in and the towns where my maternal and paternal grandparents had lived.

In very short order, the lay of the land was clear to me. All roads were now connected. What I didn't count on was the metaphor.

As I watched the numerous seniors that lived in the towns, I thought they could have been my parents. From my vantage point behind the wheel, there was little to differentiate them. They had gotten jobs, lifted themselves from poverty, survived the Depression and the war, and raised their families the best they could. They did what they knew how to do at the moment they did it. Just like my parents. Just like all the rest of us.

Suddenly everything became clear. Yes, all roads were now connected. My life and what I did with it had nothing to do with my parents. I had hung on to the narrative of self-pity and victimization for so long that I believed it all.

In an instant in that taxi, the universe said to me, "You know how all the roads are connected. Now go have your own life." Within a few months I was enrolled in a Ph.D. program, determined to put in place all of the pieces I had been neglecting, all the ones I had feared.

My parents were not "perfect," but, then, whose are? The problem didn't lie with them; it was driven by my interpretations. As a kid, I didn't know how to interpret. As an adult, I had a responsibility to reinterpret.

I choose to believe that I had the best parents in the world, because they did the best they could. The rest is up to me.

And I choose to believe the day in the taxi was all about forgiveness, a letting go of perceived slights inflicted by others as well as my own self-inflicted harms. It was about taking a big step across the threshold of the fear prison I had built. It was about coming to terms with the idea that I am 100% responsible for the choices I make.

How did it happen? Look at the previous 48 Lessons. That was the foundation. Once I stopped avoiding life's lessons, once I stopped feeling sorry for myself, once I changed my mind, I changed my life. It didn't happen overnight, but it happened. And it's still happening.

TAKEAWAY: We hold the key to our prison door and there is no lock. Forgiveness helps us see the door is ready to be opened.

Lesson 50
Stay on the Path

God will not have his work manifest by cowards.

~ Ralph Waldo Emerson

I think a spiritual journey is not so much a
journey of discovery. It's a journey of recovery.
It's a journey of uncovering your own inner nature.
It's already there.

~ Billy Corgan

I love telling the story of a man I'll call John D.

I first met John in January 2013 when he attended my Emotional Intelligence class. "I really need this class," he said. "It's coming at the right time in my life." He was pale, obese, and exhausted.

Two months later, John attended my Time Management class. During the break he told me his story. "I'm that guy who does only eighty percent of a job. My wife is always pissed at me. I always wanted to be a broker but I never studied for the exam because I listened to the pessimism and negativity of people around me."

He told me that at one point he had "dug up the bushes around our house to plant new ones and never finished it. After your class in January, I went home and finished it. I come outside and find my wife sitting there. I asked her, 'What are you doing?' She said, 'I'm just sitting here admiring the beautiful work you've done.'"

"Since January, I've lost 30 lbs. and I've decided that I will lose another 100 by April 15, 2014. In February, I took my wife and kids to the beach in Galveston.

Who goes to the beach in the winter?! We did! And it was great! I'd never done that with my family before. And what's more, I started studying for my broker's exam."

A month later I received another email from John. He'd lost 44 lbs. and was still studying. By June, he had lost a total of 50 lbs. and had revised his weight-loss goal from 100 lbs. to 150 lbs.

One weekend, he was working outside around the house, planting bushes and flowers his wife wanted. She came out and said, "What are you doing?" John replied, "I'm making those changes you asked for." She got all choked up and said, "You listened to me."

John realized he was the only one 100% responsible for his choices. He realized his fear, based on his narrative, his assumptions, and his beliefs, had been holding him back. He put some simple mechanisms in place, like the ones in this book, and changed his life.

These mechanisms are steps forward, shedding our skin of the past and stepping into who we really are.

Don't try to reinvent the wheel. Everything you need is inside you. Reach out to others to help you unlock it. If you allow yourself to be bold in overcoming your fear, you will make huge strides on your path to living the dream.

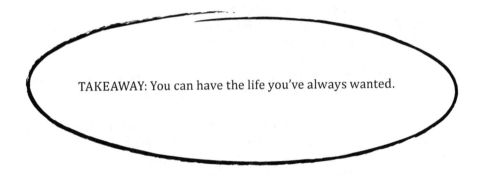

TAKEAWAY: You can have the life you've always wanted.

The Road Ahead

In three words I can sum up everything I've learned about life: It goes on.

~ Robert Frost

It is better to be hated for what you are than to be loved for what you are not.

~ Andre Gide

Let's heed the words of Robert Frost: Life goes on.

How many times have we imagined the worst possible outcome only to find that it never came to pass? How many times have we wrung our hands in worry over what others might think of us only to discover they weren't thinking about us at all? How many times have we lost time and opportunities because of the fear we created in our own minds?

As I write this, I'm reminded of the words of Mark Twain: "I've suffered a great many catastrophes in my life. Most of them never happened."

We can be our own worst enemies, failing to understand what is truly ours to own and what belongs to other people. We can be uncharitable and impatient, denying ourselves the possibility of second chances. We can hide behind gossip, blame, excuses, anger, and many other walls to avoid facing our fears.

Remember, people's opinion of us is none of our business.

I challenge you to make a Decision about how your life is going to be. I challenge you to Commit to being bold and living the dream. You have all of the tools you need to build effective mechanisms to design an amazing life – to Succeed.

So, before you close this book, write down one thing you're afraid of that you will begin addressing from today. Acknowledge your fear. Identify it. Measure it. Determine the worst case scenario. Then go out and collect information and elicit support. Reflect on your past success. And don't forget to celebrate.

You may doubt this works. You don't have to take my word for it. Re-read Lesson 50. John didn't believe it either.

You are more powerful than you imagine. You have the power to change your life. You hold the key to unlock every prison door you've created. Amazing things will happen when you do.

It all begins with you.

I would love to hear about your successes. You can reach me at drjoe@joeserio.com.

The Takeaways

Lesson 1   If you change your mind, you can change your life.

Lesson 2   It's time to change our perception of what we can handle.

Lesson 3   Instilling fear in ourselves and others does not produce the best results.

Lesson 4   Overcoming fear and moving forward is the foundation for living the dream.

Lesson 5   Build a strong Ally and put the Bully in perspective.

Lesson 6   We get to choose every day who we are.

Lesson 7   We don't have to change the world, just ourselves.

Lesson 8   Self-awareness is the critical ingredient without which little else is possible.

Lesson 9   Change begins with you. It has to start there.

Lesson 10   Don't let your insecurities cause you to jump to negative conclusions about situations.

Lesson 11   Become the Chinese farmer by living $E + R = O$.

Lesson 12   What do you believe about yourself and how is it linked to your fear?

Lesson 13   Everything we need is already here. It's time to create our belief in ourselves.

Lesson 14   We don't have to be accepted by everyone else to be enough. Being exactly who we are is what matters.

Lesson 15   Let's get off our "buts" and take charge of our destiny.

Lesson 16   Procrastination is the vicious practice of keeping ourselves from becoming ourselves.

Lesson 17   Let go of "perfect" and strive to be your best self.

Lesson 18   Don't try to give your power away to others. They actually don't want it.

Lesson 19   Choose responses that are aligned with your dreams, not your fears.

Lesson 20   A well-balanced life with the right mechanisms in place is one of the keys to success.

Lesson 21   There is no right way to achieve your goal. Work your process and stay flexible to new opportunities.

Lesson 22   Mechanisms help successful people be bold and live the dream.

Lesson 23   When we Decide and Commit, it is very difficult not to Succeed.

Lesson 24   Thinking ahead about your responses leads to new possibilities for better outcomes and a happier life.

Lesson 25   The questions we ask along the way – and the responses to these questions – influence where we end up.

Lesson 26   Honestly evaluating your life will get you further than blame and procrastination.

Lesson 27   Assessing the state of your life is a great step toward understanding your weaknesses so you can make improvements.

Lesson 28   Clarity about our positives and negatives helps drive down fear.

Lesson 29   Creating SMART goals gives your plan critical details that will optimize your chances of success.

Lesson 30   Understanding the resources we already possess helps us see how to overcome the obstacles we fear are in our path.

Lesson 31	It's your story. You get to choose if it's filled with love and happiness.
Lesson 32	Take the power out of negative beliefs by disproving them.
Lesson 33	Take time to de-clutter your space, time, and relationships in order to reduce fear.
Lesson 34	Set SMART goals to overcome fear and make progress recreating your life.
Lesson 35	Apply filters to better understand what's happening around you so you can choose the most appropriate responses.
Lesson 36	Rein in the voices in your mind so you can learn from them and change them.
Lesson 37	Understanding and welcoming plateaus is a critical part of overcoming your fear of stepping outside your comfort zone.
Lesson 38	Break down every goal or project into manageable pieces.
Lesson 39	The right tools make the job easier and lower your frustration so you're more likely to succeed.
Lesson 40	Collaboration and accountability will help you reach your goals faster.
Lesson 41	We shouldn't forsake fulfilling the potential of our lives for fear of acknowledging our fear.
Lesson 42	We must know what we're facing before we can overcome it.
Lesson 43	When fear appears, we quickly measure it in order to find the courage to keep moving forward.
Lesson 44	The fear of worst case scenarios becomes less potent when we have a plan in place and don't believe in unrealistic extremes.
Lesson 45	When we seek out information from experts and the support of knowledgeable, positive people, we set ourselves up for success.
Lesson 46	Constantly remind yourself how successful you've been so you know how capable you are.

Lesson 47   Celebrate your successes, no matter how small or inconsequential you think they are.

Lesson 48   Develop the habit of falling on your sword and taking 100% responsibility for how your life is turning out.

Lesson 49   We hold the key to our prison door and there is no lock. Forgiveness helps us see the door is ready to be opened.

Lesson 50   You can have the life you've always wanted.

Acknowledgements

A special thanks to my wife, Jennifer, without whom this book series, our business, and the wonderful life we now enjoy would not be possible. She lovingly took the manuscript in hand and applied her usual ridiculously thorough editing process to the project. She's the best partner one could ask for.

This book would not be possible were it not for the countless conversations my brother, Steve, and I have had about fear and countless related topics. The discussion began some 35 years ago and continues to this day.

Thanks to all who read the manuscript and offered feedback: Laura Atchison, Brent Boepple, Carrie Carroll, Jim Comer, Mark Cwirko, Jim Dodson, John Graham, Cherrie Greco, Roxane Marek, Stephen Plezia, Curtis Ruggles, Kim Schnurbush, Frank Serio, Grace Serio, Paul Sheldon, and Carolyn Torella.

Thanks to you for reading this book. I hope the mechanisms discussed will help you in some small way as you discover your path ahead.

Also in the *Get the Nerve™ Series*

Public Speaking:
50 Lessons on Presenting Without
Losing Your Cool

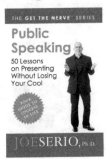

Does the thought of public speaking make you sick? Do you lie awake at night, weeks in advance of your event? Are you tired of living with the anxiety? Imagine turning all that around and feeling:

- Confident
- Calm
- Connected with your audience

Dr. Joe can help you manage your fear of public speaking so you can deliver killer presentations. In fact, as hard as it may be to believe, you can even learn to *enjoy* it.

Don't let your anxiety get in the way of your career!

ORDER NOW!

www.joeserio.com

Also in the *Get the Nerve*™ *Series*

Time Management:
50 Lessons on Finding Time for What's Important

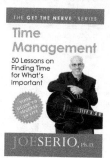

You often find yourself wondering where your time goes. Why aren't you getting done the things that are most important? Why aren't you making more progress in your career and life? Imagine having a system for turbocharging your time and feeling:

- More accomplished
- Satisfied
- Fulfilled

You can take control of your time, get organized, learn to say no more easily, and reduce the amount of stress in your life due to procrastination, perfectionism, and multitasking.

Don't let your bad time habits get in the way of your success!

ORDER NOW!

www.joeserio.com

Biography

Dr. Joe Serio is a popular and entertaining leadership trainer and conference keynote speaker who helps people and overcome barriers and improve performance. He is the founder of Law Enforcement Development Training (www.LEDtraining.com), which specializes in personal leadership programs for officers, and he is also the co-founder of The Healthy Dispatcher (www.thehealthydispatcher.com), which provides wellness training to 9-1-1 dispatchers, along with LAPD veteran dispatcher, Adam Timm.

Dr. Joe holds a Ph.D. in Criminal Justice with a specialization in Leadership and Organizational Behavior from Sam Houston State University (SHSU). As part of a unique internship program during graduate school at the University of Illinois at Chicago, Dr. Joe was the only American to work in the Organized Crime Control Department of the Soviet national police (MVD). During his stay in 1990-91, he conducted groundbreaking research on Soviet organized crime.

During this same period (1988-1993), Dr. Joe was the founding director of a summer study program at one of the five law schools in the People's Republic of China. The program included visits to Chinese prisons, neighborhood mediation committee meetings, courts, re-education through labor camps, and other criminal justice-related agencies.

In 1995-96, he worked as a Moscow-based consultant to the global corporate investigation and business intelligence firm, Kroll Associates. In 1997, he was named director of Kroll's Moscow office, where he managed a wide variety of investigations across the former Soviet Union and coordinated with Kroll offices around the world.

Dr. Joe is the author of the critically-acclaimed book, Investigating the Russian Mafia. He has delivered presentations to audiences in Russia, China, Canada, and the U.S. on Russian organized crime and security issues.

In the 1990s, he worked in Moscow as a media consultant to The New York Times, The Washington Post, CNN, BBC, and other media outlets. He helped produce three documentaries on Russian crime, including one inside Russian prisons, for the television program Investigative Reports on American cable channel A&E. He was also instrumental in producing the first-ever newspaper series on the Russian mafia. The eight-part series, "Glasnost Gangsters," appeared in the Chicago Tribune in 1991.

Dr. Joe also served for six years as editor-in-chief of the highly-regarded bi-monthly magazine, Crime and Justice International, which was produced at SHSU's Criminal Justice Center and distributed to more than 25 countries.

From 2013 to the present, Dr. Joe has been delivering conference keynote presentations to businesses, associations, and criminal justice agencies.

As a recorded musician, Dr. Serio occasionally brings music to his presentations, using harmonica and guitar to illustrate points pertaining to time management, organizational skills, and effective communication.